W9-CLQ-347

"This work is a tour de force. With his unique combination of Christian evangelical theological sophistication, clinical sensitivity and compassion, and scientific acumen and mastery, Yarhouse establishes in this compelling book why he is the most important voice reflecting on the complex challenges of sexuality today."

Stanton L. Jones, provost and professor of psychology, Wheaton College

"*Understanding Gender Dysphoria* is a deeply practical and timely book. Many of the variables surrounding the transgender community are nuanced and intense, yet completely unknown to the evangelical world. Mark provides helpful working knowledge of key terms, concepts and relevant issues. And with humility and great care he directly addresses how individual Christians and the broader evangelical church can respond. Although this book is academic in nature, it should be required reading for all church leadership. This is my new go-to book for the Marin Foundation's work with evangelicals on the topic. Mark's research must be paid attention to."

Andrew Marin, author of *Love Is an Orientation*

"This book is a must-read for pastors, educators and those who want to engage the cultural discussion around human sexuality. Yarhouse is a first-rate scholar, educator and therapist who also loves Jesus and Scripture. He deeply cares for people and the church. His approach to this complex topic is not to tell the reader what to think, but to teach the reader, who then can wisely discern how to apply the information to their particular context. This book educates so that people can lead wisely, pastor compassionately and build community that lives out the great commandment to love God and others."

Shirley V. Hoogstra, president, Council for Christian Colleges & Universities

"I deeply respect the work that Mark Yarhouse has done in this field and have benefited greatly from his thinking."

Bill Hybels, senior pastor, Willow Creek Community Church

"It's hard to keep up with current words and acronyms for sexuality and gender, much less understand what they really mean. Even more challenging is evaluating and engaging these issues from a Christian perspective. Thank God—literally and truly—for Dr. Mark Yarhouse! Yarhouse articulates a goal many Christians will quickly claim as their own: to rise above political and ideological battles to provide ministry, pastoral support and compassionate care to all persons. Yarhouse helps us begin to put this ideal into practice by explaining gender dysphoria, transgender, and gender normativity and non-normativity, based on stories, professional counseling experience and research, some conducted by him and his graduate students. He treats all persons equally, asking of us all, 'How does gender permeate our lives—and how should it?' His voice is clear and serious, his perspective well-informed and studious, and his heart pastoral and concerned for the well-being of individual persons, especially those who seek support and community within Christian churches. If you've wondered how Christians and churches can support people with gender dysphoria who are seeking a meaningful story, lifeway and community, read this book!"

Jenell Paris, professor of anthropology, Messiah College

"Speaking as a pastor to church leaders, I enthusiastically commend my friend Dr. Mark Yarhouse for his unflinching courage, heartfelt compassion, biblical loyalty and rigorous scholarship in addressing the painfully complex and controversial issue of gender dysphoria. This book is an exquisite gift of understanding that I believe is absolutely essential to the church's crafting of ministry to hurting people that reflects the grace and love of Jesus. Unwrap and use it as soon as possible!"

Andrew McQuitty, author of *Notes from the Valley*

"Mark Yarhouse has written yet another important contribution to the church's discussion about LGBTQ issues, this time focusing specifically on questions related to transgender people. This book is informed by studious attention to the Bible, sound theological reasoning and deep psychological wisdom, all of which is sifted through a compassionate heart that wants to see people experience the deep love of Christ. This book is a must read for any Christian who wants to think Christianly about what it means to be transgender. Mark's pastoral posture and commitment to biblical truth is a model for every evangelical Christian."

Preston M. Sprinkle, vice president, Eternity Bible College Boise extension

UNDERSTANDING
GENDER
DYSPHORIA

NAVIGATING TRANSGENDER
ISSUES IN A CHANGING CULTURE

MARK A. YARHOUSE

IVP Academic

An imprint of InterVarsity Press
Downers Grove, Illinois

InterVarsity Press
P.O. Box 1400, Downers Grove, IL 60515-1426
ivpress.com
email@ivpress.com

InterVarsity Press® is the book-publishing division of InterVarsity Christian Fellowship/USA®, a movement of students and faculty active on campus at hundreds of universities, colleges and schools of nursing in the United States of America, and a member movement of the International Fellowship of Evangelical Students. For information about local and regional activities, visit intervarsity.org.

All Scripture quotations, unless otherwise indicated, are taken from THE HOLY BIBLE, NEW INTERNATIONAL VERSION®, NIV® Copyright © 1973, 1978, 1984, 2011 by Biblica, Inc.™ Used by permission. All rights reserved worldwide.

While any stories in this book are true, some names and identifying information may have been changed to protect the privacy of individuals.

Cover design: Cindy Kiple
Interior design: Beth McGill
Image: clothes hanger: © fimkaJane/iStockphoto

ISBN 978-0-8308-2859-3 (print)
ISBN 978-0-8308-9860-2 (digital)

Printed in the United States of America ∞

Library of Congress Cataloging-in-Publication Data

Yarhouse, Mark A., 1968-
  Understanding gender dysphoria : navigating transgender issues in a
changing culture / Mark A. Yarhouse.
      pages cm
  Includes bibliographical references and index.
  ISBN 978-0-8308-2859-3 (pbk. : alk. paper)
  1. Sex--Religious aspects--Christianity. 2. Gender identity
disorders. 3. Gender identity--Religious aspects--Christianity. I.
Title.
  BT708.Y37 2015
  261.8'35768--dc23
                                                                    2015010660

P 29 28 27 26 25 24 23 22 21 20 19 18 17 16 15 14 13 12 11 10 9

Y 39 38 37 36 35 34 33 32 31 30 29 28 27 26 25 24 23 22 21 20 19

To the church, the Body of Christ:

For wisdom in walking with those who are navigating gender identity

concerns and questions of faith. That we may all experience

the love of the Father, the peace of Christ and

the presence of the Holy Spirit.

Contents

Introduction

MOST OF MY PROFESSIONAL WORK has been in the area of sexual identity or the act of labeling oneself based on one's sexual attractions. In that area of scholarship, I try to be clear about what we know and do not know about sexual identity, while identifying ways in which current research can inform our understanding of how Christians in particular navigate sexual identity questions in their own lives.

Several years ago I was talking with a colleague who was aware of the intense level of scrutiny I receive for my work, often receiving criticism from people or organizations on both sides of the broader culture wars. I was providing a consultation for a family whose daughter was gender dysphoric. He said, "That's a good idea; maybe move into a less controversial area of work." He was serious! It was one of those funny moments because I realized he did not know how controversial the issues are surrounding gender dysphoria and transgenderism.

That has been confirmed for me as I have conducted research for this book: no one is satisfied with anyone else's perspective on the topic of gender identity. There are considerable professional and popular divisions that have made it a virtual minefield for any author who wants to step foot on this terrain.

So I want to tread cautiously.

At the same time, I have spent years now meeting with children, adolescents and adults who have been navigating gender identity concerns, and I have had the opportunity to publish one of the first studies of its kind on a sample of Christians who are transgender. With the revelation of popular figures identifying as trans (e.g., Cher's child who is a biological female and named Chastity Bono at birth and now identifies as male, Chaz Bono) and legal challenges in Christian institutions for transgender students, faculty and staff, this topic is clearly moving toward greater cultural salience.

The fact is that there is a need for a resource that is written from a Christian perspective and is also informed by the best research we have to date, as well as seasoned with compassion for the person who is navigating gender dysphoria. I thought it would be worth trying to put together that kind of resource, and the reader will be left to decide whether I have succeeded, as the whole topic is difficult to fully understand let alone explain.

One of the first times I moved from professional discussions about gender dysphoria to a more personal discussion was a few years ago. I had met an acquaintance who is a male-to-female transsexual person and a Christian and who lived not too far away. She accepted my invitation to join my family for dinner one day after church. I had not really thought much about it. My parents invited people over for dinner all the time when I was a kid growing up in Pennsylvania and Maryland. But my parents tended to invite missionaries who were home on furlough. This was going to be different, and I don't know that I thought it all through. Then, as we spoke about finalizing the invitation, I realized she was bringing her wife. I hadn't really asked much about relationships throughout our initial exchanges. As they shared with me, they were conservative Christians who had been married and raised a family together. They did not believe in divorce. At the same time, they looked like a lesbian couple. I was then beginning to appreciate how complicated this could get.

This experience, together with other personal and professional experiences, led my research group to a series of trainings and consultations around gender dysphoria and eventually the decision to conduct the study of the experiences of transgender Christians. In the course of conducting that study, we asked several questions of participants to ensure that they were Christians—questions about what being a Christian meant to them and so on. When I presented the results at the Virginia Psychological Association, I found myself presenting the gospel as I read through the content analysis of how participants responded during that part of the interview. Participants referenced a personal relationship with Jesus, recognizing Jesus as their Savior, and so on. At a talk I gave recently on gender dysphoria, a person in the audience challenged the assumption that the people were *really* Christians: "But how do you *know* they were Christians?" he asked. "Wouldn't they just be saying what they thought you wanted to hear, to be included in the study?" I suppose so. That is always a consideration when conducting research. People can misrepresent themselves. But if we took out of every textbook every study that relied on that kind of self-report, we would have pretty thin resources, at least from the behavioral and social sciences. Back to the presentation: The majority of participants denoted starting a personal relationship with Jesus through being saved by grace through faith, thus claiming a conversion experience that is consistent with truth claims that are central tenets of Christianity. It was rather remarkable, really, and it was humbling to me as a Christian and as a researcher.

This book invites Christians to reflect on several issues related to these findings, a broader research literature I will attempt to explain, and other anecdotal accounts. I would like the reader to gain greater insight into the experiences of people who navigate gender dysphoria, recognizing that there is no one story that can capture the range of experiences that exists today. In the opening chapter, I introduce the reader to the language, categories and key terms associated with the topic. I also note that as we wade into this particular pool, we are going to quickly be in the deep end, as the topic is complex.

The second chapter helps us think through a biblical perspective on gender dysphoria and transgender issues more broadly. I look at the biblical passages that are frequently cited in these discussions. It is here that I also introduce the reader to three different frameworks or lenses through which the topic can be seen: the integrity framework, the disability framework and the diversity framework. In addition, I introduce an integrated framework that draws on the best of each of the other frameworks.

Chapter three looks at the debates about causation. There has been a recent attempt to offer a unifying theory of causation (i.e., the brain-sex theory) that captures our current interest in biological explanatory frameworks. Proponents of the brain-sex theory have been criticized by proponents of other theories, and vice versa. I essentially conclude that we would do well to humbly admit that we do not know at this time what causes gender variance or transgender experiences, including transsexuality, which has been the primary focus of research to date.

Chapter four explains the phenomenology and prevalence of gender identity issues. I review the current *Diagnostic and Statistical Manual of Mental Disorders, Fifth Edition* (*DSM-5*) diagnostic criteria for Gender Dysphoria. Although the diagnosis of Gender Dysphoria (previously Gender Identity Disorder) is rare, recent research suggests gender dysphoria may be experienced along a continuum and that the various expressions of gender variance that fall under the umbrella of transgender are more common.

Chapter five considers issues related to prevention and treatment, particularly when gender dysphoria rises to the level of a diagnosable condition. There are a considerable number of debates here, particularly whether gender dysphoria resolves naturally, whether it can be prevented from continuing into adolescence or adulthood, and whether it should be prevented. There are fewer debates among mental health professionals about treatment options for adults, although there are several paths adults take when they are navigating gender dysphoria, such as resolving to live according to one's birth sex, managing dysphoria or expressing one's preferred gender identity intermittently, or full-time cross-sex typed identification.

Chapter six brings all of what we have covered into a Christian response to gender dysphoria. The focus in this chapter is at the level of the individual, as I discuss how to respond at the level of the individual in clinical practice and ministry contexts.

The last chapter looks at how the church positions itself in relation to the broader culture with respect to gender dysphoria and transgender issues. This is particularly complicated, as the topic of gender dysphoria is subsumed under the transgender umbrella that has been closely associated with the topic of homosexuality. The church has struggled in the twenty-first century with how to conceptualize some of these concerns, as well as how to be a unified witness in the area of sexual ethics. At the level of the institution, there is a question as to what it means to be missional as a church given the dramatic changes in our culture within the past several decades.

I would like to acknowledge the many reviewers who provided me with feedback on earlier versions of the manuscript. I sought out people I knew who were familiar with the topic of gender dysphoria either personally or professionally. The range of perspectives is noteworthy and included transgender, genderqueer, and transsexual persons, each of whom is a Christian, as well as gay and lesbian Christians, and scholars and pastors who are straight and have never experienced gender dysphoria to my knowledge. Specifically, I would like to mention Trista Carr, Stanton Jones, Judson Poling, Julie Rodgers, Melinda Selmys, Sandra Stewart, William Struthers, Caryn LeMur, Peter Ould and Amy Williams. The final version is not one any of the reviewers would necessarily endorse, and I take responsibility for it as they were generous with their time and their suggestions, many of which (but not all) were incorporated into the final manuscript.

1

Gender Identity, Gender Dysphoria
and Appreciating Complexity

INTRODUCTION

On May 30, 1926, George Jorgensen Sr. and Florence Jorgensen welcomed their son, George William Jorgensen, into the world. Danish Americans who had married only four years earlier, they would christen George Jr. in the Danish Lutheran Church a few weeks later.[1] George Jr. grew up in New York City and graduated from Christopher Columbus High School in the Bronx. He was considered rather slight and frail and interpersonally shy. George Jr. avoided rough-and-tumble play, sports and other stereotypically male interests. He would go on to study photography at Mohawk College in Utica, and did a brief stint in the military. He later received training at a medical and dental assistance school in Manhattan.

Growing up in New York, George Jr. often felt that he had some kind of sexual and emotional disorder. In search of answers, he would investigate possible explanations by scouring books and articles at the New York Academy of Medicine library. His fear was he was homosexual; after all, he was sexually attracted to men. However, that did not appear to explain everything. George Jr. eventually experimented with the female hormone estradiol, and he learned during this time about a possible intervention taking place in Sweden that extended his experiments into a more meaningful and satisfying resolution. He went overseas and eventually found Dr. Christian Hamburger, an endocrinologist who was willing to provide him with hormonal replacement therapy. George Jr. would later have his testicles and penis removed; he also had vaginal plastic surgery. In 1952, George Jr. changed his name to *Christine* Jorgensen out of respect for Dr. *Christian* Hamburger.

We are talking about the 1950s. This course of events would make headlines. Indeed, the *New York Daily News* banner headline read in all capital letters: "EX-GI BECOMES BLONDE BEAUTY: OPERATIONS TRANFORM BRONX YOUTH." Although Christine was not the first person to undergo sex-reassignment surgery, she noted in her autobiography that she was the most well known at that time.

Gender identity concerns were not that well understood in the 1950s. Frankly, they are not that well understood today. There are many questions left unanswered about what causes a person to have the psychological experience of being born in the wrong body.

Controversies also exist in the area of treatment or care: How should parents respond when a child displays behaviors more characteristic of the opposite sex? Should cross-gender identification be redirected toward identification with one's birth sex? Should cross-gender identification be encouraged for a child who is already gender dysphoric? Should puberty be delayed to provide time for that kind of decision making? Or what options exist for teens and adults? Should they be encouraged to enter into therapy to resolve the conflict through psychological intervention? Is cross-gender identification to be avoided, or should it be facilitated? When people have tried different interventions, what has been helpful? What are the reasons people pursue hormonal treatment and sex-reassignment surgery? How often are these procedures helpful to people? What are the long-term effects of these kinds of interventions?

These are remarkable complicated questions that deserve our attention.

We are no longer answering these questions in a cultural context of the 1950s. One difference we can all acknowledge is that our culture has shifted toward more supportive and varied sexual and gender identity labels and communities that are very accessible to people and their families. There have certainly been increased attempts to understand and respond to this often bewildering experience.

The changing culture can be seen in both professional and popular treatment of the phenomenon. In the professional literature, the *Diagnostic and Statistical Manual of Mental Disorders, Fifth Edition* (DSM-5)[2] reflected a shift away from Gender Identity Disorder toward the use of the phrase Gender Dysphoria[3] to reduce stigma. Actually, several steps in the new nomenclature were intended to reduce stigma. The first is the shift from an emphasis on identity as the disorder to the emphasis on the dysphoria or distress associated with the gender incongruence for many people who report it. The other was the wording to allow for someone to no longer meet criteria following a transition.

Our culture has in some ways moved past the afternoon television shows that capitalized on "shock and awe" in their presentations, where you might see producers orchestrate a dramatic confrontation between a male-to-female transgender person who once dated a woman and is now surprising her with her true sense of self. These colorful presentations in the media were once an expression of almost gawking at the phenomenon, but they did not represent the kind of cultural sea change that would soon follow.

The shift in the popular media can also be seen in journalism. A few years ago Barbara Walters aired a special in which she interviewed a young bio-logical male who was being raised as a girl.[4] In discussing the decision of the parents to raise their son as a daughter, there was tremendous compassion generated around the challenges those parents and that family faced. In that same story, Walters interviewed an adolescent female who identified as male (or, more accurately, as a female-to-male transgender person). Walters inter-viewed his parents and they shared the challenges they faced, particularly for the mother in terms of wanting this to resolve in a way that would return her daughter to her. These are heartbreaking stories and challenging for everyone involved.

In response to this increased coverage, I asked the questions above: When a child is gender dysphoric, how should parents respond? Should parents raise a gender dysphoric child in the identity of the child's biological sex? Should they facilitate cross-gender identification? Or should they take a "wait and see" posture with the assumption that the right direction for that child is what will unfold?

In addition to questions about gender dysphoric children, What are the obligations for employers who have transgender employees? How should bathrooms be designated? Should medical coverage extend to hormonal treatment and sex-reassignment surgery? What about room assignments at campgrounds and at colleges and universities? What about hiring policies at churches, faith-based ministries, and at Christian colleges and universities?

As churches consider relating to a dramatically changing culture, what steps should be taken to reach unchurched persons who identify as transgender or who are part of the transgender community? Are there specific steps that could be considered to accommodate the experiences of gender dysphoric persons who visit churches?

In all of these discussions it should be noted, too, that the transgender experience is not one experience; it is best understood as an umbrella term for the many ways in which people might experience their gender identities differently from people whose gender identity is congruent with their birth sex. The experiences vary considerably and are only matched by presentation and expression or the living out of one's gender identity, which can range from pushing against gender norms (gender "bending") to cross dressing for sexual arousal to show/performance/ entertainment (drag) to transsexuality.

The transgender community, then, is broadly defined, and it has positioned itself alongside sexual minorities in the broader cultural discourse. Sexual minorities are people who experience their sexual identity in ways that are different than those in the majority (gay, lesbian, bisexual). When we speak of sexual minorities, then, we are typically referring to how people navigate sexual identity and convey their sexual preferences to themselves privately or to others publicly (e.g., frequently using the self-defining attribution "I am gay").

To enter into an informed discussion of transgender issues is to switch gears a little away from a discussion about sexual orientation. We can return to it, but it is not the focal point in the way it is when discussing homosexuality, heterosexuality and bisexuality.

To discuss being transgender is to discuss one's experience of gender identity, one's sense of oneself as male or female, and how that psychological and emotional experience is not aligning with one's birth sex.

BACKGROUND

To begin to understand gender dysphoria, it can be helpful to back up and discuss a broader context based on our understanding of sex and gender. When we refer to a person's sex, we are commonly making reference to the physical, biological and anatomic dimensions of being male or female.[5]

These facets include chromosomes, gonads, sexual anatomy and secondary sex characteristics.

Sex is frequently distinguished from gender. Gender refers to the psychological, social and cultural aspects of being male or female. When we refer to someone's gender identity, we are thinking of how a person experiences him-

KEY TERMS

Biological sex: As male or female (typically with reference to chromosomes, gonads, sex hormones, and internal reproductive anatomy and external genitalia).

Primary sex characteristics: Features that are directly part of the reproductive system, such as testes, penis and scrotum in males, and ovaries, uterus and vagina in females.

Secondary sex characteristics: Have no direct reproductive function, for example, facial hair in males and enlarged breasts in females.

Gender: The psychological, social and cultural aspects of being male or female.

Gender identity: How you experience yourself (or think of yourself) as male or female, including how masculine or feminine a person feels.

Gender role: Adoptions of cultural expectations for maleness or femaleness.

or herself (or thinks of him- or herself) as male or female, including how masculine or feminine a person feels. Gender identity is often associated with gender role. Gender role, then, refers to ways in which people adopt cultural expectations for maleness or femaleness. This includes but is not limited to academic interests, career pursuits and so on.

For most people, these various facets or dimensions of sex and gender align in ways that are essentially taken-for-granted realities. Most people you have met have a relatively unremarkable experience (or remarkable in the sense of all of these facets coming into alignment) of being born male or female (with the alignment of the various biological/physical/anatomical features noted above), identifying as a man or a woman, and feeling masculine or feminine within the cultural context in which they are raised.

But variations occur in these areas. For example, there is likely greater variability in how masculine or feminine a person feels, and that is often a reflection of whether they are reared in an environment with rigid gender roles and how well that person's experiences line up with those expectations.

These variations occur in other areas as well and are often discussed as intersexuality or an intersex condition.[6] In the area of biological/physical/anatomical sex, we can note several deviations from the norm of being born male or female. For example, a former client of mine had been diagnosed with

Klinefelter Syndrome, a genetic disorder of gonadal differentiation in which that person had an extra X chromosome (XXY).[7] Another person could be born with either incomplete or mixed ovarian and testicular tissues, a condition that has often been referred to previously as true hermaphroditism.[8]

Table 1.1. Physical/Biological/Anatomical Facets of Being Male or Female

Facet	Male	Female
Chromosomes	XY	XX
Gonads	Testes	Ovaries
Sexual anatomy	Scrotum, penis, vas deferens, etc.	Labia, clitoris, vagina, fallopian tubes, etc.
Secondary sex characteristics	Greater muscle mass, etc.	Wider hips, enlarged breasts, etc.

A friend of mine has yet another physiological condition—androgen insensitivity syndrome—as a result of malfunctioning gonads and other prenatal concerns. Although she does not choose to identify as intersex, many of these individuals would describe themselves that way, referring to any number of variations from the norm that make identifying as male or female problematic.

Table 1.2. Understanding Sex and Gender

Biological sex	Male	Female
Gender identity	Man	Woman
Gender role	Masculine	Feminine

Where do gender identity concerns fit into all of this? I located androgyny in between man and woman as gender identity. Androgyny can refer to not having a clearly defined sense of self as a man/woman, or it can refer to a bringing together of male/female qualities or characteristics.

Table 1.3. Exceptions to Binaries

Biological sex	Male	Intersex ← →	Female
Gender identity	Man	Androgyny ← →	Woman
Gender role	Masculine	Outside cultural norms ← →	Feminine

This book is about an experience that is different from what I have been discussing so far, although there are elements of biological sex, gender role and gender identity that are all important in the discussion. Gender identity concerns—or what we refer to as gender dysphoria—refers to experiences of gender identity in which a person's psychological and emotional sense of themselves as female, for instance, does not match or align with their birth sex as male. This would be the more common presentation, but the reverse may also be experienced: a person's psychological and emotional sense of themselves as male does not match or align with their birth sex as female.

Our illustration changes, then, to something that does challenge the binary, but it does so not by residing in between the two experiences of man/woman; rather, the experience locates itself in the other (psychologically/emotionally) in ways that are often quite difficult to fully understand or empathize with.

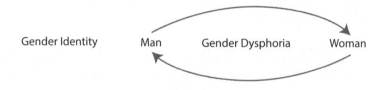

Figure 1.1.

Dysphoria means being uneasy about or generally dissatisfied with something. Thus, gender dysphoria refers to the experience of having a psychological and emotional identity as either male or female, and that your psychological and emotional identity does not correspond to your biological sex—this perceived incongruity can be the source of deep and ongoing discomfort. Specifically, gender dysphoria, is on the one hand the experience of being born male (biological sex) but feeling a psychological and emotional identity as female. Similarly, gender dysphoria is the experience of being born female (biological sex) but feeling a psychological or emotional identity as male. When a person experiences gender incongruence and it is causing them significant distress or impairment, they may meet criteria for the diagnosis of Gender Dysphoria.[9]

However, as we broaden the discussion to transgender issues, we begin to extend the discussion beyond merely the experience of gender dysphoria, an experience that might be characterized by gender incongruence in which the person does not experience an aligning of birth sex and psychological sense of gender. Transgender is an umbrella term for the many ways in which people might experience and/or present and express (or live out) their gender iden-

KEY TERMS

Gender dysphoria: The experience of distress associated with the incongruence wherein one's psychological and emotional gender identity does not match one's biological sex.

Transgender: An umbrella term for the many ways in which people might experience and/or present and express (or live out) their gender identities differently from people whose sense of gender identity is congruent with their biological sex.

Cisgender: A word to contrast with transgender and to signify that one's psychological and emotional experience of gender identity is congruent with one's biological sex.[10]

Gender bending: Intentionally crossing or "bending" gender roles.

Cross-dressing: Dressing in the clothing or adopting the presentation of the other sex. Motivations for cross-dressing vary significantly.

Third sex or **third gender**: A term used to describe persons who are neither man nor woman, which could reference an intermediate state or another sex or gender or having qualities of both man/woman in oneself.

Transsexual: A person who believes he or she was born in the "wrong" body (of the other sex) and wishes to transition (or has transitioned) through hormonal treatment and sex-reassignment surgery.

Male-to-Female (MtF): A person who is identified as male at birth but experiences a female gender identity and has or is in the process of adopting a female presentation.

Female-to-Male (FtM): A person who is identified as female at birth but experiences a male gender identity and has or is in the process of adopting a male presentation.

Genderfluid: A term used when a person wants to convey that their experience of gender is not fixed as either male/female but may either fluctuate along a continuum or encompass qualities of both gender identities.

Genderqueer: An umbrella term for ways in which people experience their gender identity outside of or in between a male-female binary (e.g., no gender, genderfluid). Some people prefer a gender-neutral pronoun (e.g., "one").

Drag queen: A biological male who dresses as a female (typically flamboyant dress and appearance) for the purposes of entertaining others. Such a person may not experience gender dysphoria and does not tend to identify as transgender.

Drag king: A biological female who dresses as a male (stereotypic dress and appearance) for the purposes of enter-

> taining others. As with drag queens, such a person may not experience gender dysphoria and does not tend to identify as transgender.
>
> **Transvestism**: Dressing or adopting the presentation of the other sex, typically for the purpose of sexual arousal (and may reflect a fetish quality). Such a person may not experience gender dysphoria and may not identify as transgender. Most transgender persons do not cross-dress for arousal and see transvestism as a different phenomenon than what they experience.
>
> **Intersex**: A term to describe conditions (e.g., congenital adrenal hyperplasia) in which a person is born with sex characteristics or anatomy that does not allow clear identification as male or female. The causes of an intersex condition can be chromosomal, gonadal or genital.

tities differently from people whose sense of gender identity is congruent with their biological sex.

A person could be under the transgender umbrella and be gender dysphoric (experiencing significant incongruence that is distressing). Another person could cross-dress and find the act of cross-dressing sexually arousing (but they might not experience the gender dysphoria the other person reports). Still another person could cross-dress with a strong desire to start hormonal treatment with an eye for sex-reassignment surgery. Yet another person could do drag shows and be quite flamboyant in presentation (e.g., drag queen or drag king), which may have little if anything to do with a subjective experience of dysphoria or a desire for sexual arousal. That person would unlikely identify as transgender, although some might, and that person's decision could be tied to motivations to cross-dress in this manner.

It should be noted that not every expression of gender variance defined in the sidebar would report gender dysphoria. Most people who have an intersex condition, for instance, do not experience gender dysphoria, although they have a higher incidence rate than those who do not have an intersex condition, and many would report going through a time of navigating gender identity questions.[11] Likewise, most people who perform in drag would not report gender dysphoria as such and may not identify themselves as transgender—nor would those who do identify as transgender necessarily consider those who perform drag to be transgender.

If you are beginning to get the sense that this could get complicated, you are not alone. This is an area that requires time and patience to unpack and truly understand—and even then, we do so with humility given how much we do not know at this time. But the church is going to need to spend some time on this topic. I urge church leaders to spend time in careful reflection as we think about the best way to engage the broader culture from more of a missional approach while simultaneously considering how to come alongside people within our own Christian communities who are navigating this terrain.

TOWARD A REASONED RESPONSE

This brings us back to the person. I am thinking here of the person who is navigating gender identity questions in his or her life. I am thinking of the person who experiences gender dysphoria. That experience of gender incongruence—the experience of biological sex and psychological experience of gender not aligning—can also be experienced along a continuum. In other words, gender identity concerns are not one thing experienced in exactly the same way by all people everywhere who experience it. Rather, think about the experience of incongruence and distress/discomfort reflecting different degrees of both incongruence and discomfort.

What is the best way to proceed for the person who experiences gender dysphoria? The remainder of this book takes that into consideration, but let me outline a few things for us to consider as we move in the direction of a more thoughtful response.

Let's consider what we have said so far: the person is navigating gender identity concerns. These concerns are real and often quite confusing and isolating. The person worries about who would believe them, what people would think about them, and so forth. This is tremendously isolating and often associated with other concerns, such as depression and anxiety. One reviewer shared with me that she had a good friend who cross-dressed and abused a significant amount of alcohol to suppress her dysphoria; she shared that the substance abuse abated once her friend was able to come to a place of congruence.

This is also not a particularly common concern. Most people experience a remarkable alignment of the many facets that make up biological sex and their sense of themselves as male or female. But for those who experience gender identity conflicts, the church will need to consider how best to respond.

At the level of the individual, it can be helpful to ask a simple question, such as: How is the gender identity conflict experienced by this person? Invite the person to tell you more about their experiences.

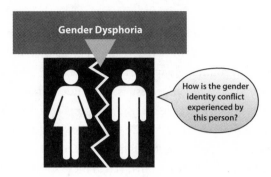

Figure 1.2.

Keep in mind, too, that the person is navigating gender identity questions in a cultural context in which many people will respond to them out of a culture war mentality. No one navigates gender identity concerns in a vacuum. Rather, each person who faces this unique challenge does so in a sociocultural context in which sex and gender are being discussed and debated.

As I mentioned earlier, some people are capitalizing on discussions in this area to deconstruct sex and gender. I will discuss this in greater detail in chapter two. David Kinnaman of the Barna Group, in discussing gay marriage and reflecting on our rapidly changing culture, observed that

> the data shows that evangelicals remain countercultural against a rising tide of public opinion. If the sands have shifted under evangelicals' feet in the last 10 years, we at Barna predict it will seem the ground has completely opened be-

Figure 1.3.

neath them during the next 10. In part, that's because the very belief that same-sex relationships are morally wrong is deemed by many to be discriminatory and bigoted.[12]

This comment by Kinnaman is in reference to same-sex sexuality, but the overarching discussion is about LGBT issues in general. In other words, the cultural opinion surrounding gay marriage represents a broader cultural opinion that extends to transgender issues and gender variant persons. These cultural shifts frequently trigger a response from social conservatives of concern and, in some cases, fear for the erosion of long-held norms. These battles are played out in politics, entertainment, the media and education. The person you are talking to is unlikely involved in these spheres but may simply be looking for support as they navigate this terrain.

As Christians provide care to people in a sociocultural context characterized by ideological and political battles, we need to think about rising above the culture war when providing ministry and meaningful pastoral care and support. We keep it in view (it is inescapable) while we provide services and compassionate care.

Why is this important? There is good reason to believe that the next generation of Christians tends to value a relational ethic that does not sacrifice relationships even when drawing distinctions in ethics and morality:

> The Christian response to these issues [marriage, ethics, human flourishing, and so on] has to be rooted in a deeply relational ethic—that sexuality is a relational and interconnected aspect of our humanity. That relationships matter, including those between people who disagree.[13]

We will want to keep this in mind, and this book is intended to respect that shift in how discussions are carried out between people where there is disagreement, but it is at least important to recognize this cultural shift among Christians.

Unfortunately, one way people respond to transgender issues is to devalue the person who is gender variant and simultaneously turn to rigid stereotypes of gender. That reaction is not only overly restrictive, but it can create a forced choice for those who do not fit into those rigid categories. It won't be helpful to stress stereotypes that people are unable to adopt. Also, keep in mind that we have witnessed a cultural shift that may contribute to greater uncertainty around sex and gender.[14]

Also, I will share later some thoughts and suggestions on what it looks like to live out various expressions of gender identity concerns, but generally speaking, I can see the value in encouraging individuals who experience gender identity conflicts to resolve the conflicts in keeping with their birth sex if possible. Where those strategies have been unsuccessful, I recognize the potential value in managing the gender identity conflict or concern through the least invasive means (recognizing surgery as the most invasive step toward expression of one's internal sense of identity). I will come back to this, as it warrants more attention. There is a risk, too, with so much media attention focusing almost exclusively on transsexuality while there are many other expressions and experiences of transgenderism and gender variance. I will say this for now: *Given the complexities associated with these issues and the potential for many and varied presentations, pastoral sensitivity should be a priority.*

Also, I know many people who are navigating gender identity concerns who love Jesus and are desperately seeking to honor him. I think it would be a mistake to see these individuals as rebellious (as a group) or as projects. Some do identify as transgender or use other labels or ways of naming their reality, and I would like the church to provide a supportive environment for them as they navigate this difficult terrain.

Rather than reject the person facing such conflicts, the Christian community would do well to recognize the conflict and try to work with the person to find the least invasive ways to manage the gender identity concerns. I will return to this principle throughout the book, but the idea is that there are many ways in which a person who experiences gender identity concerns along a continuum might manage experiences of gender dysphoria. Just as the experiences reside along a continuum, so too do the possibilities for exploration of identity and management of what contributes to gender dysphoria.

CONCLUDING THOUGHTS

Gender identity concerns remain one of the most complex and difficult to fully understand. We know so little about the etiology and best course of care, though there are strong proponents for different theories and approaches, and there is division among mental health professionals on some important points and between some mental health professionals and some members of the transgender community. We will discuss each of these issues in greater detail in subsequent chapters.

When the topic of treating gender dysphoric children is brought up, some professionals focus on resolving gender dysphoria to reach congruence with the child's birth sex. This has been increasingly viewed with skepticism; vocal critics from the transgender community have expressed how this is not unlike conversion therapy for homosexuality. Also, once a child reaches late adolescence or adulthood, there are few large-scale studies of psychosocial interventions toward this end, and even less optimism for such a resolution once a person has reached adulthood. Perhaps as a result, the field has moved in the direction of support for those who wish to pursue cross-gender identification, with several models that either "wait and see" or facilitate such cross-gender identification through puberty suppression. Once a person reaches adulthood, consideration is then given to medical interventions to facilitate cross-gender identification, and these may include hormonal treatment and sex-reassignment surgery.

As we close this chapter, I want to point out that there has been one study published of male-to-female transgender Christians.[15] It noted conflicts with gender identity and religious identity in terms of personal faith, God and the local church.[16] Interestingly, some transgender Christians shared that their gender dysphoria led to a *strengthening* of their personal faith; others reported a *past struggle* with their faith, and still others left the organized religion with which they grew up. For some, the challenges they faced brought them closer to God, but others reported a strained relationship with God because of their gender dysphoria. Particularly common was past conflict with the local church community or the persons and leaders who represent these organizations. I will return to this study throughout this book, as some of the information shared in that context may inform our broader discussion.

It is unclear to me at this time whether there is any one outcome that is ultimately satisfying to everyone who has a stake in these discussions. It is such a rare condition that we have little good research from which to draw strong conclusions, and I have known people who felt gender dysphoria so strongly that they felt nothing less than their sanity and their life was at stake. They desperately sought a resolution to the dysphoria that caused them significant distress and impairment. This is not an argument that they should pursue the most invasive procedures, but we also acknowledge that we understand and empathize with that decision, as painful as it often is. Rather than reject the person facing such conflicts, the Christian community would do well to recognize the conflict and try to work with the person to find the least invasive ways to manage the dysphoria. Perhaps future programs of research will provide greater insight and clarity into an area that seems particularly difficult to navigate at this time. These include but are not limited to research on the types of resolutions sought by people with an eye for the developmental considerations associated with gender dysphoria in childhood, adolescence and adhulthood, how strength of gender dysphoria is related to various attempted resolutions, the role of personal values and religious faith commitments in seeking resolutions, and so on. There is an opportunity here to learn much more than we know at present, and we would do well to enter into the discussion with patience and humility as we balance multiple perspectives on how best to resolve what people often report to be an impossible situation.

2

A Christian Perspective
on Gender Dysphoria

INTRODUCTION

A few years ago I was presenting on gender dysphoria to a large group of Christian leaders when a hand shot up in the back of the room. I asked the gentleman if he had a question. He did. Opening his Bible, he stood up and cleared his throat, creating a pause that heighted the expectations the audience had for what he might say. He then paraphrased 1 Corinthians 6:9-10, and asked, "What do you do with the Word of God, which clearly says 'neither the effeminate . . . shall inherit the kingdom of God'?" This was a rhetorical question. He closed his Bible and sat down as if to say, "That covers it. We are done. The matter is closed."

It is one of those difficult moments in public speaking. As the person conducting a workshop, it is tempting to use the platform to take on a person who takes a position intended to close down the discussion. However, I have never wanted to interact with an audience in that way. When I have made the mistake of using the stage toward that end, I have always regretted it. Also, in this case, he and I have in common a high regard for Scripture. I thanked him for his commitment to the Word of God. I appreciated that his reference point was Scripture as an important resource in any discussion about matters of life and faith and ministry. I fully intend for it to be a reference point for me too.

The question that arises is: *In what ways does the Bible speak to this issue of gender dysphoria?* I am not asking whether it has any relevance. I am an evangelical Christian who affirms that Scripture is a reliable guide for the believer. The Bible is "fully truthful in all its teachings."[1] It is, then, a "sure source of guidance"[2] in matters of faith and life. I affirm that view of Scripture and hold it in high regard. It is precisely because Christians hold a high view of Scripture that we want to come to it with respect for what it addresses and how it informs our present concerns. That is certainly the case as we turn to the topic of gender dysphoria.

There is a need to balance between two hazards when we turn to the Bible to inform our discussion about gender dysphoria. The one hazard is to look to Scripture for answers it is not prepared to provide.[3] The other hazard is to fail to critically reflect on the sociocultural context in which we live and make decisions about gender identity and dysphoria.

Let's look at the first hazard. As I think about gender dysphoria as a condition diagnosed by mental health care professionals in the twenty-first century in the West, it is hard to know how to apply some of the biblical references to sex and gender.

In part because of the connections often made between the transgender community and the gay community (or lesbian, gay, bisexual and transgender [LGBT] community), people often ask, Is gender dysphoria like homosexuality? If the traditional Christian sexual ethic views same-sex behavior as a moral prohibition, does this prohibition extend to transgender issues and, if so, how? Put differently, should gender dysphoria be approached like a predisposition to behavior that falls in a category of moral evaluation in the way that Christians might discuss same-sex behavior? Is it like homosexuality in some important ways?[4] The moral equivalent, then, would be a concern for cross-dressing activities and the potential desire for and use of hormonal treatment and sex-reassignment surgery, let alone questions of sexual intimacy and relationships.[5]

The second hazard is to fail to appreciate and therefore critically engage the sociocultural context in which we live and make decisions about gender identity and dysphoria. I have already discussed gender dysphoria as a mental health issue that is a diagnosable condition (Gender Dysphoria). For some Christians, that will place the topic squarely in a frame away from sexual morality per se and into the realm of how mental health professionals think about these concerns. However, we can also recognize that Christians might not view mental health issues and moral issues in the same way the broader culture views these issues.[6] It might not be enough to just point to a diagnostic manual for confirmation that an issue is strictly a mental health concern and that it has nothing to do with moral and ethical considerations.

Where does that leave us? There is a tremendous opportunity—as we keep these two hazards in view—to offer a thoughtful, informed reflection on the ways in which Scripture enters into our discussion. What I want to do first is look at some of the common biblical passages that are cited with reference to this topic. Then I will move the discussion toward the broader themes where we can have more confidence in what God is saying to us about gender dysphoria. For this we will look at creation, the fall, redemption and glorification.

FREQUENTLY CITED BIBLICAL PASSAGES

Let me go back to the gentleman who stood up and paraphrased 1 Corinthians 6:9-10. Remember that he said, "neither the effeminate . . . shall inherit the kingdom of God." As I shared with him and others present, I read that passage as being about the man who is passive in a same-sex sexual encounter and not specifically speaking to the topic of gender dysphoria or transgender issues.[7] The primary moral concern is with same-sex behavior, and while cross-dressing may have played a role in that context, it is less clear to me that specific dress and appearance was the primary concern or the moral prohibition having to do with sexual activity.

It is possible that both are a concern, and my overall thought is that this gentleman brings up a good point. What does Scripture say? How do we read Scripture and avoid the two hazards I described above?

More so referenced than the 1 Corinthians passage is a passage from Deuteronomy. It is not uncommon in discussions about gender dysphoria and transgender issues for interested parties to point to Deuteronomy 23:1, which says, "No one who has been emasculated by crushing or cutting may enter the assembly of the LORD." Likewise, Deuteronomy 22:5 reads, "A woman must not wear men's clothing, nor a man wear women's clothing, for the LORD your God detests anyone who does this."

As I shared earlier, an argument can be made that there is an integrity associated with our maleness and femaleness, something essential and sacred that is ultimately bumped up against in the experience of transsexuality. At the same time, thoughtful Christians have reflected on these same passages and the scope of Scripture and encouraged us to be cautious about making too strong a declaration. For example, in their discussion of these and other biblical passages, the Evangelical Alliance Policy Commission notes that Deuteronomy 23:1 and Deuteronomy 22:5 are commonly referenced by Christians who are looking for a biblical perspective on transgender concerns. However, they are concerned that such an appeal often reflects "simplistic moral readings of the Bible that treat it as a sort of ethical cookbook."[8]

The EAPC notes "a clear progression in Scripture which culminates in the implied acceptance of the genitally-mutilated by Jesus in Matt 19:12, and the conversion, baptism and acceptance into the Kingdom of God of the Ethiopian eunuch in Acts 8:26-39."[9] In the context we have (answering a question put to him about divorce), the Matthew 19 passage, insofar as it references those who "choose to live like eunuchs," almost certainly refers to those who choose not to marry (rather than suggesting they were castrating themselves).[10]

These passages appear to reflect a concern that the ancient Israelites not participate in rituals that were practiced by the Canaanites:

> It is likely that, in keeping with God's covenantal concern to preserve the holiness of his character reflected within the covenant community of Israel, and to avoid anything which threatened Israel's existence and harmony, the cross-dressing prohibition was introduced to prevent involvement on the part of the Israelites in contemporary Canaanite religious rituals of the day, which involved swapping of sex roles and cross-dressing.[11]

The EAPC offers a further sobering reflection tied to the meaning of the words in Deuteronomy 23:1: "Nevertheless, the strength of the Hebrew word translated as 'abomination' or 'detests' indicates that in the sight of God such practices were fundamentally incompatible with the identity of God's people."[12] Other passages, such as Deuteronomy 22:5, were likely "intended to signify a reaffirmation of divine intent, in that the sanctity of the distinctiveness between the two created sexes is to be maintained."[13]

The passages from Deuteronomy are certainly important, and we can see different ways in which we might understand them. We can also see that even where we might demonstrate some restraint and caution, we see a reaffirmation of gendered distinctiveness that Christians would want to understand and support.

In addition to these passages from Deuteronomy, the other passages that we need to discuss have to do with eunuchs. The EAPC mentions them in conjunction with the passages from Deuteronomy, so let me come back to how we might best understand eunuchs. In Acts 8:26-40, we read about Phillip and the Ethiopian Eunuch:

Now an angel of the Lord said to Philip, "Go south to the road—the desert road—that goes down from Jerusalem to Gaza." So he started out, and on his way he met an Ethiopian eunuch, an important official in charge of all the treasury of the Kandake (which means "queen of the Ethiopians"). This man had gone to Jerusalem to worship, and on his way home was sitting in his chariot reading the Book of Isaiah the prophet. The Spirit told Philip, "Go to that chariot and stay near it."

Then Philip ran up to the chariot and heard the man reading Isaiah the prophet. "Do you understand what you are reading?" Philip asked.

"How can I," he said, "unless someone explains it to me?" So he invited Philip to come up and sit with him.

This is the passage of Scripture the eunuch was reading:

> "He was led like a sheep to the slaughter,
>   and as a lamb before its shearer is silent,
>   so he did not open his mouth.
> In his humiliation he was deprived of justice.
>   Who can speak of his descendants?
> For his life was taken from the earth."

The eunuch asked Philip, "Tell me, please, who is the prophet talking about, himself or someone else?" Then Philip began with that very passage of Scripture and told him the good news about Jesus.

As they traveled along the road, they came to some water and the eunuch said, "Look, here is water. What can stand in the way of my being baptized?" And he gave orders to stop the chariot. Then both Philip and the eunuch went down into the water and Philip baptized him. When they came up out of the water, the Spirit of the Lord suddenly took Philip away, and the eunuch did not see him again, but went on his way rejoicing. Philip, however, appeared at Azotus and traveled about, preaching the gospel in all the towns until he reached Caesarea.

A eunuch is a man whose testicles have been removed. In the biblical context, Jesus makes a rather interesting comment that I alluded to earlier about eunuchs. His comments are recorded in Matthew 19:12:

> For there are eunuchs who were born that way, and there are eunuchs who have been made eunuchs by others—and there are those who choose to live like eunuchs for the sake of the kingdom of heaven. The one who can accept this should accept it.

The mention of eunuchs in this context has been thought by some authors to be speaking of a "third sex" or perhaps relevant to gender dysphoria. I can understand the desire to see in this passage something that would help us understand these issues better; however, we have no evidence that eunuchs were either a different gender or gender dysphoric. Adrian Thatcher asserts that the eunuchs who were "born that way" refers to "people who are born with ambiguous genitalia."[14] That seems plausible; others have suggested that it could also reference some condition comparable to a diminished sexual capacity, although it may be hard to speculate beyond that. The eunuchs in these contexts were most frequently either court officials or slaves.[15]

Thatcher also discusses those who castrate themselves for the kingdom of God. He argues for three ways to approach the text: (1) literally, though he is rightly skeptical of the claim that these would be people who actually as a group castrated themselves; (2) metaphorically, by which it would mean "have renounced marriage,"[16] but Thatcher is unconvinced; and (3) hyperbolically, as an exaggeration that ultimately points to a "training of the will" or "a life of sexual self-restraint."[17] There may be something to this last consideration, although I think the more common interpretation of renouncing marriage is a reasonable interpretation and has historically been compelling to many Christians.

Taken together, what can we conclude from these passages of Scripture? First, let me say that I rarely like to cite a passage as a quick way to respond to a complicated topic. It never seems to do justice to the complexity. I think we do better to look at broader biblical themes that help us develop our thoughts and inform a Christian worldview. At the same time, theology should not be so sophisticated that a person could not come to a basic understanding of God's will by a reading of his Word. If you are working really hard to make sense of a passage that is relatively clear, it might be that you are looking to justify something rather than really apply the obvious meaning of the text to your present circumstances.

As I read these passages, I find myself unconvinced that they alone provide the final word on the experiences of gender dysphoric persons or persons who are navigating gender identity conflicts. The passages seem to speak to a cultural context in which Israel was to be set apart from the pagan practices of their neighbors.[18] At the same time, part of what was being practiced by pagans did seem to push back against a created order in a way that should give the believer pause. It may not be a moral concern in exactly the same way that same-sex sexual behavior is a moral concern, but is there a sense in which cross-dressing for the purposes of deconstructing sex and gender should be a concern to the Christian? I think so, but it is difficult to get much more from isolated passages like these without doing a fair amount of hermeneutical gymnastics to advance an argument on either side of the culture wars. What we do see in Jesus is a way in which he approached and interacted with eunuchs. Those exchanges are not directly related to gender dysphoria (although some expressions of what we refer to as gender variance were likely present during biblical times), in my view, but they do show a compassion that I would like to see characterize the local church.

Also, I appreciate what Looy and Bouma had to say in their reflection on the nature of gender in their analysis of the experiences of intersexed and transgender persons:

> Gender is a good and vital aspect of human nature, but it is not all of human nature. Gender also does not reflect a *straightforward* division of humankind into two subspecies. Both within and transcending gender is much psychological, behavioral, and even physical diversity.... Further, ... sin has distorted both physical experiences and cultural expressions of gender.[19]

As Looy and Bouma suggest, the experiences of transgender persons "create for all of us a tension between healthy diversity and the distortion of sin, and call us to reflect on how we should understand gender in light of the essential Christian motifs of creation, fall, and redemption."[20]

THE FOUR ACTS OF THE BIBLICAL DRAMA

What I find more informative than some of the specific verses cited above is to think about sexuality and gender in the context of God's redemptive plan for creation. That redemptive plan is frequently discussed with reference to the four acts of the biblical drama: *creation, the fall, redemption* and *glorification.*

Creation. Christians have historically understood the creation story to say something significant about God's purposes for sex and gender. The creation story presents us with Adam and Eve as delighting in their physical existence as gendered persons. We can affirm the goodness of our physical existence, including what contributes to our experience of our sex (as male and female) and gender.

As we think about extending that observation of the goodness of our physical existence and ourselves as gendered persons, one distinction that may be helpful is to recognize different aspects of our sexuality: *gender sexuality, erotic sexuality* and *genital sexuality.*[21]

Gender sexuality is the broadest of the three levels. It refers to being a person who is either male or female. Christians have historically understood there to be two biological sexes, and gender sexuality is a reflection of that distinction and complementarity seen in the creation narrative (Gen 2:21-24). By saying this, I am in no way meaning to diminish the experience of those who have an intersex condition or experience gender identity concerns, and some would say such rare conditions or experiences are exceptions that perhaps prove the rule, that is, that there are two distinct and complementary sexes, just as we see reflected in the story of creation.

Erotic sexuality and *genital sexuality* are the other two types of sexuality. Erotic sexuality refers to the passionate desire and longing for completion in another. The longing for completion is experienced at all levels, including the physical. Erotic sexuality is related to gender sexuality for most people.[22] The complementarity of male and female anatomy certainly reflects this, but same-sex partners can also experience a longing for completion in the other that reflects this level of erotic sexuality.

Genital sexuality is comprised of and focuses upon physical acts themselves.[23] It is probably the focal point of most evangelical Christians when they discuss sex—which behaviors are acceptable and which are unacceptable? What is right and wrong in terms of sexual behavior? These are important questions to ask, of course, but our discussion requires a broader, fuller view of sex and gender to inform a Christian understanding of gender identity concerns.

According to Jones, questions for Christians for reflection include, Why did God created two sexes? What was God's purpose in so doing? What are the meaningful differences between men and women, if we can tease those out from our sociocultural context? Also, how does our gender permeate our lives as we live after the fall and before glorification? How ought gender permeate our lives?[24]

The view that "gender enables unity," that is, that "man and woman become 'one flesh'" is an important biblical theme from creation that should inform our understanding of redemption.[25]

We can only speculate as to why God created two sexes. Obviously, God did not have to create the world the way that it is. But God chose to create two sexes. We do see examples throughout the Old and New Testaments that suggest that the coming together as male and female, as a man and a woman in marriage is meant to signal something of the relationship between God and his people (Old Testament) and between Christ and the church (New Testament). This is probably one of the most common themes throughout Scripture and positions God in relation to a community that is being redeemed. The relationship between God and the people of God is an intimate one, a covenantal one, steeped in significance, purpose and meaning.

To be human is also to experience a longing for completion. Did God create us with a longing for completion that forces us to look outside of ourselves so that the longing itself would be illustrative? It may be that the longing for the other that is related to our biological sex and gendered selves—because it is meant to represent a longing for God—was made possible in the creation of two sexes and is not in any way incidental to the creation. The creation of two sexes provides, then, a living illustration of a point intended to direct us toward our Creator.

Christians can make these observations about sex and gender differences without overstating their case, which is often a temptation. It is difficult to tease out the real and meaningful differences between men and women. Neural mapping of the brain suggests differences between males and females that are particularly significant at adolescence and into adulthood: "The observations suggest that male brains are structured to facilitate connectivity between perception and coordinated action, whereas female brains are designed to facilitate communication between analytical and intuitive processing modes."[26]

But many differences between men and women are not categorical; rather, they are better viewed as two bell-shaped curves in which the average experiences of men and the average experiences of women are different, while having considerable overlap either in ability or with reference to a characteristic. Indeed, "all of the research on gender differences in various personality traits, cognitive abilities, and preferences consistently shows that, even when there are statistically significant differences between women and men, these differences pale in magnitude beside the variations among women and among men."[27] It is rather artificial to focus on the differences between men and women and may unnecessarily create a false dichotomy through "such narrow definitions of what it is to be female or male that virtually all of us fall short of the 'ideal' or the prototype."[28]

It is also quite possible that when we look at the question, *Why did God create two sexes?* we may not be able to look to scientific findings for any definitive answer, and perhaps that is appropriate and significant. The answer may reside in theological anthropology. Christopher Roberts puts it this way: "[Is] the human body theologically significant in its sexual features? . . . If it is, how will these features participate in our redemption? What is the relationship between our bodies, our desires, and our true selves?"[29] In his concluding thoughts about the significance of sexual difference, Roberts writes, "[Human] beings are ontologically (and not merely in appearance) male and female, and so their deepest fulfillment will come through forms of life that welcome this difference and are structured upon it."[30]

Heather Looy, in offering some tentative considerations about the image of God in her discussion of intersexuality, offers that it is possible that

> the "genderfulness" of God [may have been] deliberately separated into female and male by God in the creation of humankind as a way of structuring into creation a basic need for us to be in relationship, so that it is in community, not individually, that we most fully reflect God's image and are most fully equipped for the tasks to which we are called.[31]

This is a fascinating consideration, and in my view, it deserves more time and attention. Is it possible that we see in the differences between male and female a separation of what Looy describes as the "genderfulness" of God? Are we created in a way that highlights diversity in our very being and ways of relating to one another as gendered beings? It is certainly a compelling view and vision for our experience of interrelatedness.

For our purposes, we are left with the question, *How does gender permeate our lives—and how should it?* That is another challenging question for the Christian community. Christians can affirm two different sexes and recognize that we are to relate to one another as gendered selves. However, our gender identity and gender roles are often shaped by our current cultural context, the messages we receive about what it means to be a man or a woman, and the standards by which we frequently compare ourselves. We want to avoid adherence to rigid stereotypes of what it means to be male or female; we want to recognize a range of experiences of our gender and ways of relating as gendered selves through various norms and roles that can be described along a continuum.

The fall. Christians also look at the reality of *the fall.* It is important to consider that original sin has corrupted all of existence, including human sexuality and experiences of our gendered selves. The consequences of the fall are far-reaching, but we get glimpses into the purpose of sexuality and its complementarity in what God chooses to reveal about his relationship with Israel. Indeed, God reveals a very intimate relationship with his people by equating Israel to a wayward wife who prostitutes herself with others while God is a faithful husband. (Also, in this analogy God is the husband, and in the New Testament Christ is the bridegroom, which places all Christians [no matter our gender] as female in how we as the church relate to God, which can be a little confusing to some men in the church who might not readily identify with this role and way of relating to God.)

As we think about the three aspects of sexuality—gender, erotic and genital sexuality—we see that the fall can affect biological/physical/anatomical sex and gender. Here are a few of the potential effects. I noted previously any number of departures from the norm that can be found in biology, from Klinefelter Syndrome (in which the person has an extra sex chromosome, XXY) to Androgen Insensitivity Syndrome (in which a person has external female genitalia and an outward appearance as female but XY male chromosomes). Other experiences include congenital adrenal hyperplasia (CAH), which can have many outcomes but could include XX chromosomes but male external genitalia. CAH is "the result of an enzyme deficiency (most commonly 2 1-hydroxlase) that occurs in both males and females" . . . and "is inherited as an autosomal recessive disorder."[32] These are effects of the fall at the level of the chromosomes, the gonads, and testicular or ovarian tissues, among other things.

An important consideration from the outset, then, is that Christians do not affirm that every experience—that every biological or psychological reality—is a reflection of God's will.[33] No one and nothing is free from the effects of the fall, although the fall touches our lives in remarkably different ways. The world we inhabit, as well as our experience of ourselves (our bodies, our minds) are not as God intended.

If what we experience around us (in the world) and within us (in our bodies and our minds) are not exactly as God intended, how should we think of ourselves? Well, one word that comes to mind is that we are *disordered.*[34] I think this word captures the human condition. However, there are two concerns I have about the word. First, I do not want the word to be used to focus in on certain experiences to the exclusion of our own disorder. In other words, when we speak of being disordered, it should be noted that we share with one another this essential quality; we do not focus on the disorder of the other while overlooking our own disorder before a holy God.

A second concern I have is that the word is likely to create misgivings even among Christians who are also navigating gender identity concerns. Let me draw a parallel to the experiences Christian sexual minorities have. We see an increasing number of gay Christians—even conservative, celibate gay Christians who prefer to use the word *gay* rather than *homosexual* or *same-sex attracted* to capture their experience. In a post in which she reacted to the language of homosexuality being "intrinsically disordered," Eve Tushnet wrote:

> If sexual desire can be easily tweezed away from nonsexual longing and love and adoration then yeah, sure, I guess I can see the point of calling homosexual desire "disordered." But that's not how *eros* actually works! My lesbianism is part of why I form the friendships I form. It's part of why I volunteer at a pregnancy center. Not because I'm attracted to the women I counsel, but because my connection to other women does have an adoring and erotic component, and I wanted to find a way to express that connection through works of mercy. My lesbianism is part of why I love the authors I love. It's inextricable from who I am and how I live in the world. Therefore I can't help but think it's inextricable from my *vocation*.[35]

There is an entire debate about language and identity among conservative Christians about whether gay Christians should refer to themselves as such. I am not going to enter into that debate here. I have discussed my thoughts elsewhere.[36] But the challenge exists insofar as gender and gender identity are significant meaning-making structures that inform our sense of self and our way of relating to those around us. We relate to one another and to God and to the world around us as gendered selves. We will have to be thoughtful in how we reference the fall in our understanding of diverse experiences of gender identity that do not match up well with a gender binary. Those who experience their gender identity differently than in more stereotypical roles and expressions likely experience their gender identity as who they are and as a way for them to serve others and to know God.

Having said that, I acknowledge that we are—all of us—disordered. We do not like to think of ourselves as disordered, and this too is a reflection of the fall. The noetic effects of sin are seen in the disorder in our own minds (Rom 1:18-23) and in our knowledge of God and the world God created, including ourselves. O'Donovan puts it this way: "Together with man's essential involvement in created order and his rebellious discontent with it, we must reckon also upon the opacity and obscurity of that order to the human mind which has rejected the knowledge of its Creator."[37] I think it's important, then, to realize any discussion of disorder is unlikely to be embraced. It is a hard reality that each of us faces. What will make it harder is if we treat gender dysphoria as disorder while those of us who do not experience gender dysphoria or do not relate to one another outside of a gender binary relate to others as though we are not ourselves disordered.

We usually think of disorder as a word reserved for more extreme conditions or experiences, such as significant depression or anxiety that keeps us from going to work or being present to our kids. We think of disorder perhaps in medical conditions, such as cancer or heart disease. But all of it is disordered. Even the healthiest of us is still living in a fallen world as a fallen person.

The fall will touch our lives in ways that vary significantly from person to person. One person may be susceptible to depression in a way that another person is not (based on family history). Likewise, a person could be at greater risk for heart disease because of family history. My uncle suffered from schizophrenia for over thirty years. He was perhaps at greater risk for it than someone else, but he certainly lived with a debilitating mental health condition that is a reflection of the fall—the world and the way we experience it is not as God originally intended.

How do gender identity concerns fit into this picture of a fallen world?

I think the fall can be seen in the lack of congruence between birth sex and psychological sense of gender identity, particularly when this is strong enough to cause distress and impairment. In those instances (and I recognize it may be difficult to draw any kind of line here), this incongruence may very well be a reflection of our fallen world. But it is not quite that simple. As Looy and Bouma observe, Christians may affirm that sex is dichotomous, but it becomes more complicated when we move to assert that gender identity is also fundamentally dichotomous, that "there is an essential female and male mind and spirit that complement and complete one another."[38] How much of what we think of as essential is acculturation as male or female?

What does the assertion of an essential female and male mind/spirit even mean? We may make a lot of differences between the sexes, but as I noted earlier, the group differences among males and among females are much more noteworthy than the differences between the two groups (between males and females). I am not saying that there are no differences in gender identity, but the underlying assumption of a fundamentally dichotomous gender identity difference may not be as helpful and may lead to a kind of rigid stereotyping that could actually exacerbate questions about gender identity.

The tendency to move toward rigid stereotyping of dichotomous gender identity differences has to be held in tension with our current sociocultural context in which sex and gender as fixed categories are being deconstructed. That is, the idea that they are norms or standards is being challenged in favor of a genderless society, which I will discuss further below. Christians can note that there is a difference between recognizing exceptions to binaries (and offering a thoughtful, compassionate pastoral response to those for whom this reality is quite salient) and arguing that the sex binary is arbitrary, socially constructed or oppressive. Quite the contrary, the Christian argues that the sex differences are instructive.[39]

While I am on the topic of deconstructing sex and gender, I should note that most transgender people I have known are not in favor of a genderless society. Quite the opposite: they favor a gendered society, but they long for a sense of congruence in which their body and their mind align. This is especially true for those who identify as transsexual. Most are not meaning to participate in a culture war; most are casualties of the culture war. Younger people in the transgender community may be landing more in the area of genderqueer or genderfluid in ways that may challenge assumptions about a sex binary extending toward a gender binary in any fixed or rigid way.

So members of the church who do not experience gender dysphoria should not assume that all transgender persons want to deconstruct sex and gender per se. There are voices in our culture that do want that, to be sure. But the average person who identifies as transsexual is unlikely to be that person.

However, most people sorting out gender identity concerns do so in a cultural context in which a culture war has been taking place. On the one side are those who view sex and gender as more or less arbitrary and a reflection of authority structures (including religious authority) that needs to be challenged and ultimately defeated. The goal there is to deconstruct sex and gender. On the other side are those who oppose such a direction. They view sex and gender as meaningful categories that, at least in the case of sex, are tied to essential aspects of what it means to be human.

Where are Christians in this mix? Some Christians have entered into the culture wars, while others have focused on what they see as other ways to witness to the culture. While this is not a book about the culture wars, what I would say is this: Christians often react to the deconstruction of sex and gender, and they should offer a reasoned response to it (i.e., retain convictions) in a spirit of mutual respect (i.e., with civility)[40] and a pastoral heart of compassion. They would do well to offer a thoughtful response rather than a knee-jerk reaction, particularly when there are people within our own communities who are navigating these gender identity concerns in their own lives. If the church only responds in the larger context of a culture war, we are going to have real casualties—people who see the church as interested in defending their turf rather than coming alongside those who are on the margins.

Moreover, Christians can do more than just avoid being culturally reactive. We can be proactive. We can listen to the person who experiences gender dysphoria. We can come alongside them and remain in a sustained relationship even when things are unclear for us or when we do not know what to say. Some churches will feel called to be more missional to a changing culture. They will approach unchurched and dechurched persons—including those who experience gender dysphoria—from a much more open and welcoming position in which any person entering their community will be made to feel welcome and connected to others. I will discuss this further in chapters six and seven.

Redemption. As we move in our discussion of the fall toward the theme of redemption, we recognize that God does not leave humanity in its fallen condition. A proper understanding of redemption and glorification is essential to understanding a Christian approach to the world around us, to ourselves, to the question of gender identity and dysphoria. Scripture reminds us that God does not abandon us in our fallen state. Rather, God steps into our fallen world through the incarnation, through the person of Jesus, and he fully intends to redeem believers, to sanctify or make them holy, to set them apart for his purposes.

To think in these terms, we want to then consider our *telos* and our place and purpose in creation. As O'Donovan puts it, "Abstraction from teleology creates a dangerous misunderstanding of the place of man in the universe. For it supposes that the observing mind encounters an inert creation—not, that is, a creation without movement, but a creation without a point to its movement."[41]

A Christian perspective on gender identity and gender dysphoria sees these topics in the context of God's redemptive plan—with an eye for the direction and purpose of our very existence. When a person's symptoms rise to the level of a diagnosis of Gender Dysphoria, they contend with a specific cluster of symptoms that are identified in the contemporary nomenclature of mental health concerns, in ways that are not unlike how other people contend with issues that make mental health and well-being difficult for them. Some struggle with anger. Others struggle with lust that takes the form of sexual addiction. Still others struggle to delight in their relationship with their spouse, their children, or their neighbors or coworkers. Each of these is an expression of how our mental health and experience of well-being is not what God intends for us. They are expressions of our state. In response to this state or condition and in support of a direction and purpose, Christians ought to restore one another. Christians hold out hope that God is at work redeeming these experiences and believe we glimpse something of a future glory with him when we see gains made in our experiences of mental health and well-being.

Glorification. The fourth act of the biblical drama is tied to redemption insofar as it asks the teleological and eschatological question, *What is creation moving toward?* We are not offered much by way of a look into the eschaton. Jesus is recorded as saying we will not marry in heaven (Mt 22:30), but that is not to say we will have a "genderless existence": "He does not say there will be no gender in heaven, but only that there will be no marriage as we have in this life on earth."[42] I like the way O'Donovan notes that "humanity in the presence of God will know a community in which the fidelity of love which marriage makes possible will be extended beyond the limits of marriage."[43]

Also, we are given an image in the New Testament for the church, and that is of a bride. In this intimate relationship, Jesus is the groom (Eph 5:31-32). This same image is offered again in the presentation of the New Jerusalem (Rev 21:2, 9). Although we do not want to read too much into this, it raises the question of whether these images "form a timeless analog, underscoring the lasting value of and perhaps a divine purpose behind human gender" insofar as

maleness and femaleness forever defines an important aspect of the relationship Christ has to all of us, his church. How our individual gender identities will play out in the eschaton is not revealed, but God wants us to forever think of our relationship with Jesus through a monogamous, male/female relational analogy.[44]

When we look at church history, we see little initial focus on sexual differentiation in the early Christian tradition. According to Roberts, what may have been rather unclear comes into greater focus with Augustine, who believed that "sexual difference is an ontologically significant feature of humanity in every era of theological history, from creation to eschaton."[45] Indeed, Augustine suggested that "sexual difference will be adapted to some new use in heaven, in the eschatological era when marriage is obsolete."[46] Both Luther and Calvin would extend this discussion of the importance of sexual difference, placing a greater emphasis on marriage than celibacy, but asserting that "sexual difference is a fundamental aspect of being human, regardless of whether one is married or not."[47]

To return to the present, Christians ought to thoughtfully discern God's will because—from the perspective of the eschaton and of glorification—we are moving toward a time when all we will know is conformity to God's will:

> When we speak of Christian morality in relation to the kingdom of God . . . we assert the same dependence of the present upon the future. The conviction of a final triumph of God's will, in which every other created will is conformed to it, makes sense of our present relative and imperfect commitment to doing God's will. . . . We do not even pretend to describe what the life of perfect participation in the restored order of creation will be like; for the only model for such a description was concealed from our sight by a cloud at the point of his glorification, so that the apostle must say that although we are now children of God, it has not yet been shown us what we shall be (1 Jn. 3:2).[48]

From this brief sketch of a Christian understanding of the biblical drama we see that an understanding of sin brings with it a corresponding affirmation of the *inherent goodness of creation*. A Christian perspective also affirms that the inherent goodness is *tainted and incomplete in some ways*. So there is a need to balance key doctrines about personhood with each of the four acts of creation, fall, redemption and glorification. Again, each of us is created in the image and likeness of God and therefore of infinite worth. Further, sexual difference is from creation and has been a part of Christian thought as ontologically significant and in some ways a living parable about the relationship between God and his people. At the same time, Christians recognize that we are marred by the fall—we are broken, incomplete and disordered persons. However, the reality of redemption and the hope of resurrection tells us never to give up and that God's grace is sufficient to cover all of what we may encounter (including our own wrongs) if we are in a right relationship with God.

DIFFERENT FRAMEWORKS FOR CONCEPTUALIZING GENDER IDENTITY CONCERNS

As we look at the available evidence from Scripture—specific passages and the various themes that arise from reflecting on the four acts of the biblical drama—we are left with the question of how the Christian is to engage the work being done in the area of gender incongruence or gender dysphoria. I have found it helpful to distinguish three different frameworks for understanding gender identity concerns; these function as three lenses through which people view the topic.

The integrity framework. The first lens is what I refer to as the *integrity* framework. This lens views sex and gender and, therefore, gender identity conflicts in terms of "the sacred integrity of maleness or femaleness stamped on one's body."[49] Cross-gender identification is a concern in large part because it threatens the integrity of male-female distinctions. Proponents of this view would cite many of the biblical passages I mentioned above (e.g., Deut 22:5; 23:1). Even if there was some concession that some of the Old Testament biblical prohibitions were related to avoiding pagan practices of their neighbors, the overall themes from Scripture support the importance of complementary male-female differences from creation (e.g., Gen 2:21-24).

The theological approach that is at the foundation of the integrity framework raises similar concerns about cross-gender identification as are raised about homosexuality. In other words, from this perspective same-sex sexual behavior is sin in part because it does not "merge or join two persons into an integrated sexual whole"; the "essential maleness" and "essential femaleness" is not brought together as intended from creation. When extended to the discussion of transsexuality and cross-gender identification, the theological concerns rest in the "denial of the integrity of one's own sex and an overt attempt at marring the sacred image of maleness or femaleness formed by God."[50]

Language that refers to maleness and femaleness as "sacred" may be unfamiliar to some readers. In the integrity framework, this language is appropriate and comes in part from Genesis 2:21-24, which refers to woman being formed from a part of the "earth creature" ('*adam*, related to '*adamah*, "earth, ground"), the Hebrew term used, though commonly translated "rib" in this passage, refers nearly everywhere else in the Old Testament to "side" of sacred architecture: the ark, tabernacle, incense altar, temple rooms. The implication is that to tamper with one's creation as male or female (here by seeking to mask or even put under the knife one's embodied masculinity or femininity) is sacrilege.[51]

Theologically conservative Christians will resonate with this framework. To them, the integrity framework most clearly reflects the biblical witness about sex and gender and becomes the primary lens through which they view gender dysphoria and transsexuality. While it may be challenging to identify a "line" in thought, behavior and manner that reflects cross-gender identification, there becomes a point at which the integrity framework is concerned that cross-gender identification moves against the integrity of one's biological sex, an immutable and essential aspect of one's personhood.

As I mentioned above, other issues arise when we discuss the idea of maleness and femaleness and how we respond in the context of a fallen world. Recall Looy and Bouma's reminder that while gender is both "good" and "vital" it is also only a part of human nature and that the variability seen here is further complicated by ways in which the fall distorts "both physical experiences and cultural expressions of gender."[52] But the integrity framework is an important contribution to this discussion, as it reminds us of God's creational intent and is the primary (or even exclusive) lens for most evangelical Christians.

A caution to those who adhere to the integrity framework is the risk of overstating the case—that is, to promote the view that "gender and sexuality were designed in a particular manner for particular purposes implies a universality and stability that discounts the constantly shifting diversity that we observe and experience."[53]

It should be noted that many people, some Christians included, do not view gender dysphoria or transsexuality or every experience of cross-gender identification as an extension of homosexuality in precisely this same way. They may be uncomfortable with cross-gender identification or have reservations about the more invasive procedures (e.g., sex-reassignment surgery), and they may not have another way to conceptualize the phenomenon. However, from a theological perspective and in terms of a traditional Christian sexual ethic, they do not reach the conclusion that the experience of gender dysphoria or attempts to mitigate the dysphoria belongs to the same class of behaviors that are deemed immoral.

The disability framework. A second way to think about gender dysphoria is with reference to the mental health dimensions of the phenomenon. I refer to this as the *disability* framework. For Christians who are drawn more to this framework, gender dysphoria is viewed as a result of living in a fallen world in which the condition—like so many mental health concerns—is a nonmoral reality. Whether we consider brain-sex theory or any other explanatory framework for the origins of the phenomenon, the causal pathways and existing structures are viewed by proponents of the disability framework as not functioning as originally intended. If the various aspects of sex and gender are not aligning, then that nonmoral reality reflects one more dimension of human experience that is "not the way it's supposed to be."[54]

There are different ways to think about various mental health conditions as nonmoral realities. For example, is the diagnosis of Gender Dysphoria more like what we see with an eating disorder, like anorexia, a condition that has multiple contributing factors in terms of causation and maintenance but is thought to be significantly influenced by the sociocultural context in which we reside today? Or is the diagnosis of Gender Dysphoria more like a depression associated with differences in levels of serotonin, so that biology makes a significant contribution but so do other factors that could contribute to and certainly maintain the concern? Or could it be like schizophrenia that is thought to be largely based on biological contributions and not as clearly tied to culture as such?

Yet a preference for seeing the diagnosis of Gender Dysphoria as a disability of some kind still raises many questions about etiology, prevention, maintenance, and treatment and care. There are many kinds of "disabilities," if you will. There are many paths to disability as well.

My point at present is that, in each of the above cases, we do not think of personal morality as the reference point when we think of the mental health condition. Also, we do not tend to reference morality when we focus on treatment (whether curative or palliative) in terms of whether a person eats or views themselves as too fat when they are below their weight for their body size and type. Nor do we view a person's depression as sin or a person's struggle with schizophrenia as sin. Rather, they contend with a condition made possible in light of the fall. The person may have choices to make that are associated with their response to symptoms or overall treatment approach (again, whether curative or palliative), and those choices may have moral and ethical dimensions, but their condition is not one they chose; that is, they are not morally culpable for having it.

Those who are drawn more to this framework seek to learn as much as can be learned from two key sources. The first source is special revelation, and I am thinking here of meaningful themes regarding sex and gender from Scripture. The second key source is general revelation. Here I am thinking of research on etiology, prevention and intervention, as well as the lived reality of persons navigating gender dysphoria. The care provided would be through a lens of compassion and empathy. The question then arises, *How should we respond to a condition with reference to the created order, the reality of the fall and the hope of restoration?*

Evangelical Christians may recognize that the disability framework may be of some limited use, but they will likely have reservations depending on the primacy of the integrity framework. Evangelicals recognize that we live in a fallen world and that every aspect of the created world is touched in some way by the fall, so they can see how gender dysphoria could be one such manifestation. They may recognize the utility of the disability framework insofar as the person has not chosen to experience gender dysphoria, and the disability framework evokes in the Christian a greater sense of compassion and empathy.

The challenges that arise for those who are drawn to the disability framework are twofold. First, proponents of the disability framework may value the sacredness and ontological significance of male and female differences (implied in conceptualizing gender dysphoria as a disability or as aspects of personhood not functioning properly).[55] However, the openness to palliative care and interventions that allow for cross-gender identification may not be a sufficient response to adherents of the integrity framework. As Looy points out in her discussion of intersexuality, those who look at these conditions as a reflection of the fall tend to appeal to God's original intentions for sex and gender in their pastoral care: "While the fall into sin has created distortions in how femaleness and maleness are experienced and expressed, living in the time of grace means that we must seek to redeem gender and sexuality in harmony with God's intentions."[56] As we saw with our discussion of the integrity framework, such a view adds both "a theological and a moral dimension" to the discussion.[57]

Second, in so doing, Christians who utilize the disability framework are not where proponents of the diversity framework will want them to be (as I will discuss below). That is, they are still discussing gender dysphoria as a disability, which does little to provide the kind of meaningful identity and community support found in the diversity framework.

The diversity framework. A third way to think about transgender issues is to see them as something to be celebrated, honored or revered. The sociocultural context in which we live in the West is rapidly moving in this direction. I think of this as a *diversity* framework. The diversity framework highlights transgender issues as reflecting an identity and culture to be celebrated as an expression of diversity. Current models that celebrate a transgender identity and community reflect this framework. This understanding also frequently cites historical examples in which gender variant expressions have been documented and held in higher esteem, such as the Fa'afafine of Samoan Polynesian culture and the Two-Spirit people identified in some Native American tribes.[58]

Evangelical Christians are understandably wary of the diversity framework. Evangelicals see among those who adhere to the diversity framework a small but vocal group that calls for the deconstruction of norms related to sex and gender. I describe those efforts as a *strong* form of the diversity framework (as contrasted with a *weak* form that focuses primarily on identity and community). Judith Butler, for example, represents a strong form of the diversity framework when she blurs distinctions between sex and gender:

> Is there a history of how the duality of sex was established, a genealogy that might expose the binary options as a variable construction? Are the ostensibly natural facts of sex discursively produced by various scientific discourses in the service of other political and social interests? If the immutable character of sex is contested, perhaps this construct called "sex" is as culturally constructed as gender; indeed, perhaps it was always already gender, with the consequence that the distinction between sex and gender turns out to be no distinction at all.[59]

Whereas the biological distinction between male/female had been considered rather immutable, as we can see, there are those who wish to recast sex as *just as socially constructed* as gender. From another report:

> We believe it is indispensable to deconstruct the binary sex/gender system that shapes the Western world so absolutely that in most cases it goes unnoticed. For "other sexualities to be possible" it is indispensable and urgent that we stop governing ourselves by the absurd notion that only two possible body types

exist, male and female, with only two genders inextricably linked to them, man and woman. We make trans and intersex issues our priority because their presence, activism and theoretical contributions show us the path to a new paradigm that will allow as many bodies, sexualities and identities to exist as those living in this world might wish to have, with each one of them respected, desired, celebrated.[60]

The concern from proponents of the strong version of the diversity framework is that the sex-gender binary is one more source of authority that needs to be deconstructed in order to create room for the various exceptions to the sex-gender binary. Proponents believe that the benefits to doing so will open up a new vista for the range of ways in which people experience their sexuality and gender. Such claims challenge not only gender norms that have been widely understood to be socially constructed but also a sex binary as something fixed and stable, tied to an essentialist view with biological foundations.

As I mentioned above, not everyone who adheres to the diversity framework is actively attempting to deconstruct sex and gender. It is hard to estimate how many people who adhere to the diversity framework represent a strong form of the framework. I suspect that those who advocate a strong form of the framework are in the minority, as those who advocate for the strong form tend to be academics who are proponents of the scholarship of Michel Foucault, Judith Butler and others. Over time, such work may reach more of a popular level and tip the balance, but for the time being, I think most adherents of the diversity framework are proponents of the weak form with its emphasis on identity and community. I have had a similar experience in my interactions with people who are gender dysphoric: they value what I refer to as the weak form of the diversity framework because they find answers to questions about identity ("Who am I?") and community ("Of which community am I a part?").

To the evangelical Christian, the strong form of the diversity framework (that advocates for the deconstruction of sex and gender) is a much more radical alternative to either the integrity framework or the disability framework. The weak form of the diversity framework will warrant more attention and consideration, but evangelical Christians will be understandably wary of any voices, however nuanced, that draw upon the diversity framework.

How are these different frameworks important as we consider a Christian worldview? It would be wise for Christians to at least recognize that these different frameworks are in play in our cultural discussions surrounding sex and gender. That is a first step—just being able to clearly identify the assumptions behind each framework and how they contribute to the larger cultural discourse.

Table 2.1. Three Contrasting Frameworks

Integrity Framework	Disability Framework	Diversity Framework
Identifies the phenomenon of gender incongruence as confusing the sacredness of maleness and femaleness and specific resolutions as violations of that integrity.	Identifies gender incongruence as a reflection of a fallen world in which the condition is a disability, a nonmoral reality to be addressed with compassion.	*Strong form*: Deconstruction of sex/gender. *Weak form*: Highlights transgender issues as reflecting an identity and culture to be celebrated as an expression of diversity.

The failure to recognize frameworks will only contribute to more caricatures of different positions without a more nuanced and accurate understanding of the different stakeholders. To the extent that Christians want to have any kind of meaningful discussion of common ground and genuine differences, there is a need for the development of cognitive complexity, which includes the capacity to see through the eyes of others. To facilitate that kind of perspective taking, it helps to recognize the appeal of the various versions of these frameworks to adherents and to a broader culture that is a witness to these exchanges.

The next step in developing a Christian response is to identify what can be learned from each framework, as well as what concerns may arise if one framework is embraced to the exclusion of the others. As I will unpack in greater detail later in this chapter and again throughout various chapters of this book, Christians can draw on the sacredness, the compassion and the identity dimensions found in the corresponding frameworks of integrity, disability and diversity. No one framework will likely be sufficient for a truly comprehensive Christian engagement.

It is problematic for the evangelical Christian to fully embrace the strong form of the diversity framework and especially the philosophical assumptions that underlie it. However, the diversity framework helps the conservative Christian understand some of the limitations of more conservative (and sometimes rigid) scripts for gender identity and roles. Furthermore, there is no way for the Christian community to understand gender dysphoric individuals without exploring elements of the diversity framework. If Christians simply shout "*Integrity, integrity, integrity!*" and "*Sacred, sacred, sacred!*"

in discussions about gender dysphoria, we will fail to appreciate ways in which these other frameworks inform how people who experience gender dysphoria navigate difficult and quite complex decisions throughout their lives. In the end, Christians who rely solely on the integrity framework may shore up borders within the local church, but we will actually fail to engage those within the broader culture who are watching these exchanges, and I suspect we will drive gender dysphoric persons away from Christ and away from Christian community.

I invite the reader, then, who might be understandably cautious, to consider what information can be gleaned from both the disability framework and even elements of the weak form of the diversity framework, particularly when it speaks to meaning-making structures for identity and community. At least commit some time to reflect on what may be lost in terms of questions that remain about compassion, identity and community, questions that I believe will be increasingly important considerations in our changing culture.

Toward an integrated framework. My concern is that any one of these three frameworks—to the exclusion of the best the others have to offer—will likely be an inadequate response for the Christian community. My own leaning is to identify strengths in each framework, to essentially see these as lenses through which we see the topic under discussion. Rather than select one lens to look at gender dysphoria, we can look through all three, identify the strengths of each framework and apply it to how we approach the topic and the person who is navigating this terrain. What we have then is what I refer to as an *integrated framework* that draws on the best of each existing framework.

For example, perhaps because of my role as a psychologist who makes diagnoses and provides treatment in the area in which gender dysphoria is presented in its most severe manifestation, I see value in a disability framework that sees gender dysphoria as a reflection of a fallen world in which the condition itself is a nonmoral reality. This helps me see the person who is navigating gender identity issues with empathy and compassion. The focus here is on how to help a person manage his or her gender dysphoria insofar as it is the result of gender incongruence.

At the same time, as we affirm elements of the disability framework, the church will want to be sensitive to ways in which the integrity framework may need to inform ministry and pastoral care. That framework represents a genuine concern from a Christian worldview for the integrity and sacredness of sex and gender and the potential ways in which maleness and femaleness represent something instructive for the church and something for which we should have high regard. The church should reject as far too reductionistic the teaching that gender incongruence is the result of willful disobedience; such

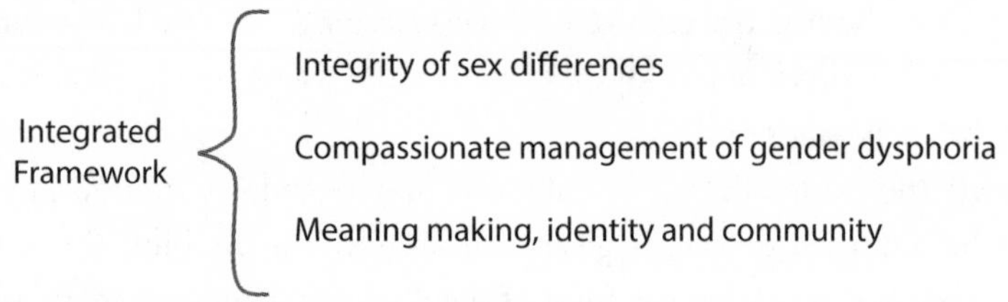

Integrated
Framework
{
Integrity of sex differences

Compassionate management of gender dysphoria

Meaning making, identity and community

Figure 2.1. An Integrated Framework

an approach avoids the hard places of ministry and shepherding and keeps the person at bay by placing the blame (and heaping greater shame) on the person navigating gender identity concerns. This is not pastoral care. The church can be sensitive as questions arise about how best to manage gender dysphoria in light of the integrity of male/female differences while recognizing that we live and relate to one another in a specific cultural context in which gender roles are conveyed, in which standards arise that can vary considerably by culture. When we consider how best to manage gender dysphoria, we can also help people do so in the least invasive way possible.

It is important for Christians to be sensitive to the ways in which the weak form of the diversity framework affirms the gender dysphoric person by providing a meaning-making structure for identity that is not found in the other two frameworks. I shared several quotes above that demonstrate that some adherents of the diversity framework (the strong form of the diversity framework) draw on philosophical assumptions that fuel an attempt to deconstruct sex and gender, but not everyone who adheres to the diversity framework has that goal in view. What I want to emphasize here is that the diversity framework speaks to identity. It validates a person's experience.

What most people who are gender dysphoric find in the church is rejection and shame—the feeling that there is something fundamentally flawed in them, that the flaw is their fault (back to willful disobedience) and that if others knew about their gender incongruence, they too would reject them. This is essentially the formula for shame, and that formula will not provide any kind of meaningful structure for identity. In that formula, the gender dysphoric person who is also a Christian or was raised in a Christian community comes across standards or rules that are related to gender identity and gender roles.

LANGUAGE AND RELIANCE ON DIFFERENT FRAMEWORKS FOR DIFFERENT PURPOSES

Sometimes people who clearly love and support one another draw on different frameworks in how they conceptualize and communicate to themselves and to others the experience of gender dysphoria and cross-gender identification. They do so for different reasons and achieve different results.

For example, in the Barbara Walters special updating the experiences of Jazz, a male-to-female gender dysphoric pre-adolescent who is biologically male and has adopted a cross-gender identification as female, there is a point at which Walters asks Jazz's older sister, "What do you explain to people about your sister?" She says, "I tell people that it's a disorder and that it wasn't . . . that it's not by choice." In response to this, Jazz shares: "Personally, I don't like that word [*disorder*] that much. I prefer 'special' or 'unique' because that's what I believe transgender is."

We see two different frameworks in this brief exchange. Jazz's older sister is drawing on the disability framework ("it's a disorder"; "it's not a choice"); Jazz is drawing on the diversity framework ("I prefer 'special' or 'unique'"). The benefit of the disability framework is that it helps Jazz's sister communicate to friends about the condition or experience of gender dysphoria in a way that maximizes the likelihood of them demonstrating compassion; it lets her explain that this is not volitional—it's not something Jazz has chosen in terms of the phenomenon itself. Appeal to the disability framework can bring forth greater empathy and compassion.

Jazz prefers the diversity framework. Her reference in the exchange is not about talking to others; she is not focusing on peer group acceptance. She is talking about self-acceptance, about how she thinks of herself. The diversity framework gets at meaning, purpose, and sense of self, identity and community. It is important to understand that the language of a "disorder" her sister uses to talk to friends is not providing Jazz with the meaning-making structures that would be as appealing for identity.

These are two different frameworks being used by different people in the same family for different purposes.

The gender dysphoric person is—by virtue of the experience of gender dysphoria—unable to live up to those standards or rules associated with gender identity and roles. That person may be told that the failure to experience the kind of congruence between one's biological sex and the psychological experience of one's gender is due to personal deficiencies or shortcomings within him or her. This is the formula for shame.

The gender dysphoric person is raised in a community in which standards, rules, and goals related to gender identity and gender roles apply.

The gender dysphoric person perceives him- or herself as not living up to those standards, rules, and goals related to gender identity and gender roles.

The failure is attributed to personal deficiencies or shortcomings.

Shame.

Figure 2.2. Shame and gender dysphoria[61]

When we look at the formula for shame and the likelihood that shame will be the primary reality for most people who are Christian or raised in the church and experience gender dysphoria, is it any wonder that people will be drawn to the diversity framework to find identity, value and self-worth?

In addition to answering questions about identity, the diversity framework also answers important questions about community. The transgender community and the broader LGBT movement and community provides answers to the questions "Where do I belong?" and "Of which community am I a part?" These are critical questions that arise out of that earlier, central question about identity: "Who am I?" and "Who else understands, accepts and validates me in substantive ways?" are critical considerations for those who experience gender dysphoria.

In a study of transgender Christians, we asked the question, "What kind of support would you have liked from the church?" These can be difficult questions to reflect on if a person has previously been hurt in the church. Sometimes answers provide a glimpse into entire stories that go untold. One male-to-female transgender Christian shared, ". . . someone to cry with me, rather than just denounce me. Hey, it is scary to see God not rescue someone from cancer or schizophrenia or [gender dysphoria], . . . but learn to allow your compassion to overcome your fear and repulsion."[62]

The meaning-making structure found in the diversity framework—particularly in contrast to the message of shame from the church—is compelling and likely to be a significant draw for support and encouragement that is being underestimated today. Also, I know several gender variant persons who reflect on God's both/and maleness and femaleness as significant to them personally. One biological female who experiences gender dysphoria and is a Christian shared with me how the insights in this area (of God's both/and maleness/femaleness) have been a blessing to her. This was not initially a blessing when she first experienced gender identity conflicts, but the blessing would come later, as she was able to reflect more on her gender identity questions, as she shared with me she had an uncanny ability to understand a female and male side of things with insights and understandings few others would experience.

This person is a good example of a Christian who would not likely on her own feel the need to identify as either male or female in terms of a gender binary. She does not reduce her sense of self, her gender roles or her gender attributes into clear-cut distinctions between male/female, between masculine/feminine. She would likely relate to others out of sanctioned categories for ease of presentation and communication but, on her own, she would likely think of herself as a person who has multiple, diverse, and complementary qualities of self/identity, role and attributes.

We will discuss the practical applications of the integrated framework later in the book. It will have to be fleshed out so we have a better sense for what it looks like to take the best qualities of each framework and apply them to a counseling or ministry setting or in the context of a small group or friendship.

CONCLUDING THOUGHTS

As we saw in chapter one, we recognize that discussions of sex refer to the biological components of chromosomes, gonads, sexual anatomy and secondary sex characteristics. Discussions of gender refer to psychological and cultural components, such as gender identity (the subjective sense of being a male or female and how masculine or feminine a person feels), sexual orientation (toward the same or opposite sex or both), and gender role (adoptions of cultural scripts for maleness or femaleness).[63] Given so many different aspects of sex and gender "it is perhaps remarkable that so many align consistently on all seven factors, thus experiencing the full, uncomplicated measure of being a woman or a man."[64]

At the same time, people do experience deviations from each one of these areas as reflected in any number of experiences or conditions. One of those people I know personally is Ella. I met Ella when she was sixteen years old. She is a biological female. She looks athletic and was involved in several sports at her high school in a small, rural town in South Carolina. She and her parents came for an extended consultation. All identified themselves as Christians. As a family, they were longtime members of a local church. Ella's mother was a hairstylist and exuded warmth and Southern charm. Ella's father was reserved and polite. Both expressed dismay at their daughter's claim that she was born the wrong sex. They did not know what to make of her statements that she was a boy. In a private meeting with Ella, I was talking to her about theories about the etiology of gender incongruence. At one point I shared, "I don't think you chose to experience your gender incongruence. It sounds like you 'found yourself' with these experiences of incongruence at a fairly young age, and that your experience of dysphoria has increased in recent years." She was stunned. I asked her about her blank expression. Ella shared, "My mom and dad have taken me to three pastors: our pastor and two other pastors he asked us to talk to. All of them said that I chose this—that I was sinning. All three said that this gender thing was a sign of my disobedience. You are the first person I've talked to who said I didn't choose to feel this way."

How do we take our theological understanding and apply it to pastoral care, ministry and/or the provision of services to someone like Ella? How are we to understand her gender incongruence? I think a more accurate theological consideration is that her incongruence is one particularly complex expression of the fallen world in which we all live. The creation story points to an experience of alignment between sex and gender that she does not experience—and may not experience this side of heaven. That alignment I am referring to would not be a fixed and rigid stereotype that few could live into, but I tend to think of that alignment as quite broad and flexible with significant diversity that the world has seen within any number of cultural contexts and varied definitions for gender roles and expression.

It is hard to fully understand the nature of the fall and how it has affected Ella. It has been suggested that there are separate dimensions of sexuality, such as the physical anatomy, hormones/endocrine system, social role, sexuality and gender identity.[65] We may have to discuss Ella's gender incongruence with some humility about how the fall has touched some of these dimensions, as well as what it means for her to respond to gender incongruence in a way that decreases her dysphoria. Further, we will have to think about how the church will be a redemptive community and resource to her.

As we think together about redemptive themes for Ella, should one of these dimensions of sexuality and gender be considered more "important" or weighted more in our discussions about gender dysphoria? Those who struggle the most to understand the strong psychological sense of being the opposite sex often give more weight to what seems to be happening deep within their mind than to other facets of sexuality and gender.

Also, our understanding of redemption is very much tied to our understanding of the fall. What we do not want to do is suggest that because experiences of gender dysphoria are not as God intended from creation that Ella has a forced choice between celebrating a diversity paradigm at the expense of the integrity of creation (the integrity framework) or embrace the integrity paradigm at the risk of gender diversity being rendered meaningless—as merely an unfortunate form of suffering that will ultimately be erased in eternity. A third way is to name meaning and purpose in all of our reality (including suffering) that is in need of redemption.

What is true about the integrity paradigm and what is true about the diversity paradigm is brought together for the Christian in the redemption of Christ. Identity is found in brokenness, as a friend of mine who has experienced, and continues to experience, gender dysphoria has shared:

> Suffering in Christianity is not only not meaningless, it is ultimately one of the most powerful media for the transmission of meaning. We can stand in adoration between the cross, and kneel and kiss the wood that bore the body of our Saviour, because this is the means by which the ugly meaningless atheistic suffering of the world (the problem of evil) was transmuted into the living water, the blood of Christ, the wellspring of Creation. The great paradox here is that the Tree of Death and Suffering is the Tree of Life. This central paradox in Christianity allows us to love our own brokenness precisely because it is through that brokenness that we image the broken body of our God—and the highest expression of divine love. That God in some sense wills it to be so seems evident in Gethsemane: Christ prays "Not my will, but thine be done," and when God's will is done it involves the scourge and the nails. It's also always

struck me as particularly fitting and beautiful that when Christ is resurrected
His body is not returned to a state of perfection, as the body of Adam in Eden,
but rather it still bears the marks of His suffering and death—and indeed that
it is precisely through these marks that He is known by Thomas.[66]

Ella's experience of gender dysphoria is a reflection of things not being as
they were originally intended to be but also not a surprise to God in terms of
God's omniscience and sovereignty. Is it too much to say that it is in this
context of suffering that both meaning and identity are found? As we think
about how redemptive themes are being written in and through each of our
lives, we have to demonstrate great pastoral sensitivity in these encounters.
Also, to become a redemptive community, the local church will have to be a
place of grace and maturity.

As Jones observes, "Resolution of . . . discord may take many forms, and
require us as humble stewards to make complex choices."[67] After we look in
the next couple of chapters at what we know and do not know about causes
and the possibility of prevention and/or resolution, we will consider what it
means to be humble stewards, as well as what it looks like to be the church in
any meaningful sense to fellow Christians who are navigating this terrain.

3

What Causes
Gender Dysphoria?

"I DON'T THINK YOU CHOSE to experience gender dysphoria," I offered slowly, looking at Jeremy who had been looking away ever since he explained how long he had felt different from other boys he knew. He hadn't held eye contact once since he began talking about the time his mother caught him dressing in his sister's clothing one day after school. He wouldn't look at me when he shared how his father confronted him that same night when he came home from work. After I spoke, he turned toward me to catch my eye, as if he wanted to confirm I wasn't just saying this to make him feel better. You see, he had been told by other Christians just the opposite—that he had indeed chosen to feel like a girl; that his experience of gender dysphoria was an act of willful disobedience to be confronted by his parents if they hoped to help him, if they hoped to save him.

When you think about it, there is something rather remarkable in the claim that an adolescent would choose gender dysphoria to make life difficult for his parents or to essentially thumb his nose at God and at creation. It must seem like a more manageable conclusion to draw than taking the time to explore the questions of etiology in any depth. While a young person could experience questions about gender identity along a continuum, and I am sure some could play out family dynamics and drama through being nonconforming in many aspects of their lives, that is not the same thing as saying a person chooses gender dysphoria.

The most concise answer to the question of causation is this: *we do not know what causes gender dysphoria.* The reality is that while there are several theories for the etiology of gender dysphoria, the cause(s) is still unknown.

As we begin to look at the question of gender dysphoria, we also have to consider: what is the nature of the dysphoria? Is it the subjective sense of gender incongruence in and of itself, or is it the subjective sense of negative affect in light of the gender incongruence? The recent entry in the *DSM-5* was intended to essentially de-pathologize the gender incongruence that is the hallmark of gender identity concerns and focus on the dysphoria itself, which is the subjective distress sometimes associated with that incongruence and the desire to live as the other sex. In this nomenclature, if that dysphoria causes clinically significant distress or impairment, a person might be diagnosed with Gender Dysphoria.

But we also see in the *DSM-5* a concerted effort to shift the focus away from biological sex to assigned gender. For example, as we look at the diagnosis of Gender Dysphoria in childhood, one of the symptoms reads,

> In boys (assigned gender), a strong preference for cross-dressing or simulating female attire; or in girls (assigned gender), a strong preference for wearing only typical masculine clothing and a strong resistance to the wearing of typical feminine clothing.[1]

A concern raised by some critics[2] is that the language change seems to be more about an intersex[3] condition in which the language of "assigned gender" is significant because the hallmark of an intersex condition is that it is difficult to identify a child's sex at birth by looking at that child's external genitalia. But to refer to assigned gender when there is no evidence that the sex of the child is anything other than what is reflected in the child's external genitalia seems out of place to critics and lends itself to contrasting socially constructed gender with the essentialism of biological sex.[4]

To return to the question of gender dysphoria, we have to at least ask if the phenomenon of gender incongruence itself is the concern and not only the emotional reaction to the gender incongruence.[5] In his prior work discussing gender dysphoric children and adolescents, Zucker[6] observes that the trajectory a child or adolescent is on constitutes a kind of impairment insofar as we can identify the end state toward which the person is moving (that is, a strong desire for hormonal treatment and sex-reassignment surgery).

Another way to look at gender dysphoria is to consider whether cross-identification is a reflection of distress in and of itself. Could it be argued, as Zucker does, that the commitment to cross-gender identification, expression and role are evidence of a conflict between one's biological sex ("somatic sex") and psychological and emotional experience of gender identity ("psychological gender")?[7] Does it matter how distressing this state is? Of course. But do we want to say that if there is no subject distress or impairment in social or occupational functioning that the incongruence is itself not a concern? I think we would have a range of answers to that question, certainly among mental health professionals and also among those who are a part of the transgender community, as well as those in religious/faith communities.

Why is this important? It is important in terms of identifying whether we have a broad cultural and professional consensus on this topic. It's not clear that we do. There are genuine disagreements among professionals about how best to conceptualize this issue, and these differences will also likely be evidenced within our broader culture and within the church.

In addition, as Christians reflect on the topic of gender dysphoria, we bring a worldview that sees a connection between the world we know and experience and transcendent purposes from creation, in the context of the fall, and through redemption and glorification. Even if the profession and the culture move toward seeing transgender issues as completely healthy and hormonal treatment and sex-reassignment surgery as preferred treatment interventions, Christians might still be concerned about that response for those who might be encourage to pursue that outcome.

HETEROGENEITY UNDER THE UMBRELLA OF BEING TRANSGENDER

As we consider etiology, we have to recognize that insofar as we are discussing transgender issues as a group of like concerns, we quickly realize that there is great heterogeneity among these different phenomena. While the focus of this book is primarily on gender dysphoria or the phenomenon in which "one's internal sense of gender does not match one's genetic gender, body, or gender role,"[8] there is a range of persons who may identify as transgender, as Richard Carroll observes:

> The clinician is now confronted with an often-bewildering array of individuals with transgender experiences, including transsexuals, transvestites, she-males, queers, third sex, two-spirit, drag queens, drag kings, and cross-dressers. The phrase "transgender experience" is currently used to refer to the many different ways individuals may experience a gender identity outside of the simple cate-

gories of male or female. It should be remembered that there are many individuals who have blended genders in some way, who never seek treatment, and who may be very comfortable with their atypical gender identity.[9]

I would add to this that these are very different experiences, presentations and motivations. There is cross-dressing behavior in and of itself. Different people cross-dress for different reasons. Some cross-dress to manage dysphoria, others to express themselves. Still others cross-dress for sexual arousal.[10] Not all of these individuals experience gender dysphoria, nor would all identify as transgender necessarily. In addition to motivation, there is the male-to-female experience of gender incongruence, which can take different forms or expressions and may well have different causal pathways. There is the female-to-male experience of gender incongruence. There are biological males and females who cross-dress privately or publicly (cross-dressers), and there are biological males who cross-dress publicly for shows (drag queens) and biological females who cross-dress publicly for entertainment (drag kings).[11]

> Ted is a thirty-nine-year-old biological male who has been growing out his hair and wearing light makeup for the past eighteen years. He finds that these rather simple steps help him manage his experience of gender dysphoria. He says he doesn't mind that people relate to him as male despite thinking of himself as essentially more genderfluid than anything else.

> Sherrie is a thirty-year-old biological female who has been cross-dressing for four years. She likes to dress in masculine, or at least androgynous, attire, and is told by others that she has a more masculine appearance and plays into various male stereotypes. She says she is most comfortable in this presentation.

> Bev is a seventeen-year-old biological female who has experienced gender incongruence for as long as she can remember. She has always been more interested in things the boys did growing up, and she has had no interest whatsoever in playing with girls. She enjoys rough-and-tumble play and identifies with many interests of the boys around her. She believes God made a mistake. She says she is a boy.

> Mike is a fifty-six-year-old biological male who has been married for thirty-three years. He and his wife have two grown children together. He believes himself to be neither male nor female. He tends not to use a gender pronoun in describing himself to others; certainly not in how he thinks of himself. He and his wife love each other and are committed to staying together, as difficult and challenging as this experience has been.

> Tom is a forty-four-year-old biological male who recently completed a transition with

the aid of his therapist, hormonal treatment and sex-reassignment surgery. He uses the name Terrie, which he has always seen himself to be. He was married for twenty years, but he and his wife were unable to continue on after he finalized his plan to transition. Although she loves her husband, she has said she cannot be in what amounts to a same-gender relationship.

There is also no guarantee that each of these has its own specific cause. It very well may be that there are multiple pathways to the same endpoint (*equi-finality*). In the case of transgender issues, the one endpoint is like saying I am going to visit the East Coast. Not only are there many ways to get to the East Coast, there are many ways to be at the East Coast (think about states that have an eastern shore, such as Virginia, Delaware, South Carolina, Florida, and countless cities that are along the coast). That is probably a better conceptual frame of reference for a discussion of both causation and destination when we think of cross-dressing, gender-bending, male-to-female transgenderism, female-to-male transgenderism, and so on.

Can any one theory really speak to the complex and diverse presentations in our culture today? No.

Most of the research on causation has focused on the experiences of trans-sexual persons. Recall that these are persons whose cross-gender identifi-cation is profound. They typically identify as the other gender and may decide at some point to pursue hormonal treatment and/or sex-reassignment surgery.

Many of the debates about causation have been between those who argue for a significant biological component that reflects more essentialist assump-tions and those who rely more on a clinical typology based on sexual orien-tation. There are also those who describe a different kind of biological contri-bution in temperament/personality that interacts with the environment in a way that contrasts with the views of these others.

As we turn our attention to the different theories of etiology, it should be noted that these debates also occur in the sociocultural context of what has been referred to as identity politics.[12] As has been well documented, much of the ground that has been gained in discussions centering on homosexuality has been due to an essentialist view of sexual orientation as something im-mutable and essential to who someone is (their identity) as a person.[13]

Nowhere have conceptual struggles over identity been more pronounced than in the lesbian and gay liberation movement. The notion that sexual object choice can define who a person is has been profoundly challenged by the advent of queer politics. Visible early lesbian and gay activists emphasized the immutable and essential natures of their sexual identities. For some, they were a distinctively different natural kind of person, with the same rights as heterosexuals (another natural kind) to find fulfillment in marriage, property ownership, and so on. This strand of gay organizing (perhaps associated more closely with white, middle-class gay men, at least until the radicalizing effects of the AIDS pandemic) with its complex simultaneous appeals to difference and to sameness has a genealogy going back to pre-Stonewall homophilic activism.[14]

Discussions centering on people who experience gender dysphoria are also moving in a similar direction in which the paradigm is one of essentialism that distinguishes types of persons: transgender rather than cisgender. Some people will use transgender to describe *how* they are ("I am a person who is transgender, by which I mean I am a person who experiences gender dysphoria") while others will use transgender to describe *who* they are ("I am transgender, a member of the transgender community").

The biological essentialism that has been associated with sexual orientation (with an emphasis on neurobiological brain differences, markers on the X chromosome, twin studies, etc.) is being discussed with reference to a corresponding essentialism associated with gender identity, particularly as it is conceptualized in the brain-sex theory, which I will discuss below.

A proper critique, however, cannot be based on how people may wish to use research in the context of a larger strategy (of, say, liberation or civil rights or identity politics) but must be understood on its own terms. What do we know about causation from the research that has been conducted so far?

This critique cuts both ways: social conservatives can also have a knee-jerk reaction to research that they believe is being used by those who are advancing a social agenda of one kind or another. Put differently, if Person A is concerned that Person B is citing research to advance the deconstruction of sex and gender norms, Person A could be equally guilty of not looking at the research, simply rejecting any and all research put forth by Person B on the grounds that Person A is against the agenda put forth by Person B.

So we face the challenge of sorting through the research findings in the context of a larger cultural war about the use of such research in policy development and various legal battles.

I will share some information on the most widely cited theories and studies while moving us toward a more integrated model.

BRAIN-SEX THEORY

The most popular theory among those who believe nature is making the significant contribution to gender dysphoria is called the brain-sex theory. It is a theory that is tied, or potentially tied, to a number of hypotheses that I will summarize below. The idea is that there are areas of the brain that are different between males and females. Researchers refer to these areas of the brain as sexually dimorphic structures. "Brain sex" refers to ways in which the brain scripts toward male or female dispositions or behaviors. Diamond explains it this way:

> Since the brain is the organ determining or scripting male or female behaviors, the term brain sex is short hand to reflect on how an individual thinks and organizes the world; whether in stereotypical male or female ways. It is certainly true that the brain is the most used sexual organ of the body and the term brain sex reflects its male or female disposition. It directs the individual to think and act more like a stereotypic male or more like a female.[15]

The background to the brain-sex theory is that scientists have established that "the presence of testosterone in utero leads to the development of external male genitalia and to a male differentiated brain."[16] But these are two distinct processes; they do not occur at the same point in fetal development. In other words, sex differentiation of the genitals and sex differentiation of the brain take place at different stages of fetal development. Proponents of the brain-sex theory identify this discrepancy as significant for gender incongruence: "As sexual differentiation of the genitals takes place much earlier in the development (i.e., in the first two months of pregnancy) than sexual differentiation of the brain, which starts in the second half of pregnancy and becomes over upon reaching adulthood, these two processes may be influenced independently of each other."[17] Is it possible, then, that "a discrepancy may exist between prenatal genital differentiation and brain differentiation such that the external genitals develop, for example, as male while the brain develops as female"?[18]

Researchers, then, look at prenatal hormonal exposure as a possible key to the etiology of gender dysphoria.

Prenatal hormonal hypothesis. Left-handedness is associated with prenatal hormonal exposure and has been a part of the discussion about etiology. The idea here is that perhaps gender identity differences are the result of differences in exposure to prenatal hormones at critical months in utero. Empirical evidence in support of this hypothesis includes findings suggesting a greater likelihood of left-handedness among transsexuals,[19] although, obviously, the vast majority of left-handed individuals are not gender dysphoric. The point is that when gender dysphoria is present, that person is more likely to also be left-handed than right-handed.

Similarly, studies of finger length ratio have suggested a difference that some scientists believe speaks to etiology. Finger length ratio is believed by some scientists to be another marker of prenatal hormonal exposure. Those who support this view cite evidence suggesting that the ratio of the index finger and the ring finger is affected by exposure to testosterone in utero. The lower this finger length ratio the greater the exposure to testosterone. There is an on-average difference in that ratio between the sexes, with males having a lower ratio than females (i.e., this finger length ratio is sexually dimorphic). Some studies[20] have provided evidence that the finger ratio of transsexual men is in the range of biological females and not in the range of biological males who are not transsexual.

Although these studies are interesting, there is research that does not appear to support the theory. For example, consider a biological/genetic female who has been diagnosed with congenital adrenal hyperplasia (CAH), a genetic condition that affects her adrenal glands' production of cortisol and hormones such as aldosterone and testosterone. Her body produces too much testosterone, which leads to her being born with ambiguous genitalia (typically an enlarged clitoris) despite having normal (for a biological female) internal reproductive structures. The point is: it is uncommon for females diagnosed with CAH to develop gender dysphoria.[21]

Neuroanatomic brain differences hypothesis. A related line of research has been in the area of neuroanatomic brain differences. This hypothesis looks at brain morphology or structure. Research has already documented differences in neuroanatomical regions of the brain between males and females. Researchers have then conducted studies to see whether areas of the brains of male-to-female transsexuals are more in the male or female range.

One area of the hypothalamus in particular has received quite a significant amount of attention. Studies of the central subdivision of the bed nucleus of the stria terminalis (BSTc), an area of the hypothalamus, has been in the female range in terms of volume of cells[22] and number of cells[23] among male-to-female transsexuals.

As we move into a discussion of this research, we should recognize that these are again typically small studies that include samples of transsexuals, most of whom have undergone hormonal treatment or have been engaging in a cross-gender role for years. But this research has been taken by proponents of the brain-sex theory as empirical support for nature rather than nurture in the etiology of gender incongruence.

Probably the most frequently cited study in this area is the study by Jiang-Ning Zhou and colleagues,[24] in which the researchers compared an area of the brain of six MtF transsexuals to the same brain region in typical/cisgender males and typical/cisgender females. They reported that this region of the brain (the BSTc) was larger in cisgender males than in cisgender females (44% larger), and that this same region of the brain of MtF transsexuals was actually within the smaller, typical female range than the male range. Despite the small number of MtF transsexuals and the fact that they had all been using feminizing hormone therapy, this study made a significant and lasting impact on how many would later argue from an essentialist position about the biological basis for transsexuality.

The next most frequently cited study in this area is the one conducted by Kruijver et al.[25] Whereas the Zhou et al. study examined the size of the BSTc, the Kruijver et al. study examined the number of cells in the BSTc area among seven MtF transsexuals and found that the neuron count was in the range of the thirteen typical/cisgender females. Again, this has been widely viewed by proponents as offering empirical support for the brain-sex theory in which the brains of transsexuals are thought to have a sex-reversed structure.

The size of and number of cells in the BSTc had been shown to be related to gender dysphoria in the Zhou et al. study[26] because it was in the female range among males who identified as transsexual females. A question that arose was this: if there is evidence of a sex-reversed structure, when does this sex differentiation actually occur?

Wilson Chung and his colleagues[27] conducted a study that looked at when the BSTc actually becomes sexually dimorphic. The researchers confirmed that the BSTc was larger (as the Zhou et al. study showed) and contained more cells (as the Kruijver et al. study showed) among men than women. Those differences, however, were noted not in childhood but in adulthood, which went against some of the commonly held assumptions at that time. The researchers were surprised by these findings: "The sex difference in BSTc volume, which reached significance only in adulthood, developed much later than we expected. . . . Therefore, marked morphological changes in the human brain, including sexual differentiation, may not be limited to childhood but may extend into adulthood."[28]

The problem with these results, say critics,[29] is that most people who experience gender dysphoria recall concerns in their childhood: "Epidemiological studies show that the awareness of gender problems is generally present much earlier. Indeed, ~67–78% of transsexuals in adulthood report having strong feelings of being born in the wrong body from childhood onward, . . . supporting the idea that disturbances in fetal or neonatal gonadal steroid levels underlie the development of transsexuality."[30]

The researchers themselves do not see their findings as ruling out "early gonadal steroid effects on BSTC functions"; rather, they point to animal studies in which the earliest effects could be on "synaptic density, neuronal activity, or neurochemical content" that affect gender identity but are not measurable in terms of the volume and number of neurons until adulthood.

Some critics of the brain-sex theory see the study as undermining the theory, while proponents of the brain-sex theory assert that the differentiation begins at an earlier stage but that what can be measured (by volume/number of neurons) will only be measurable later. Both camps (opponents and proponents of the brain-sex theory) incorporated the study into their overall view of causation.

Supporters of the brain-sex theory conclude that transsexualism is a "neuro-developmental condition of the brain,"[31] or, as Diamond puts it: transsexuality is "a form of brain intersex," citing many of the studies noted above.[32] Of those who adhere to the brain-sex theory, one variation presented by Diamond is referred to as the biased-interaction theory of psychosexual development. Here is the background to that theory:

> In general, biological factors starting from XY chromosomes produce males that develop into boys and then men with whatever characteristics are appropriately seen as masculine for society and females develop into girls and then women with whatever characteristics are appropriately seen as feminine for the same society. Differences from the usual course of development are not seen as "things gone wrong" or errors of development but as to-be-expected occasional variations due to chance interactions of all the variables involved.[33]

The background a person has is reflected in what Diamond refers to as "organizing factors" such as "genetic and hormonal influences laid down prenatally that influence adult behaviors once set in motion by pubertal or post pubertal *activation processes* or events."[34] These organizing factors predispose or influence or "bias subsequent responses of the individual; they predispose the person to manifest behaviors and attitudes that have come to be recognized as predominantly masculine or feminine."[35]

Diamond offers an extended discussion about the process and how it might relate to a person who experiences a gender identity conflict:

> Starting very early in life the developing child, consciously or not, begins to compare himself or herself with others; peers and adults seen, met, or heard of. All children have this in common. . . . In so doing they analyze inner feelings and behavior preferences in comparison with those of their peers and adults. In this analysis they crucially consider "Who am I like and who am I unlike?" Role models are of particularly strong influence but there is no way to predict if a model will be chosen, who will be chosen, nor on what basis chosen. In this comparison there is no internal template of male or female into which the child attempts to fit. Instead they see if they are *same* or *different* in comparisons with peers, important persons, groups or categories of others. . . . It is the "goodness of fit" that is crucial. The typical boy, even if he is effeminate, sees himself as fitting the category "boy" and "male" and eventually growing to be a man with all the accoutrements of masculinity that go with it. Similarly the typical girl, even if quite masculine, grows to aspire being a woman and probably being a mother. The comparisons allow for great flexibility in cultural variation in regard to gendered behaviors. It is the adaptive value of this inherent nature of brain development that trumps a concept of a male-female brain template to organize gender development.

In most cases the contributions from nature that lay out a kind of "brain template"[36] correspond with a person's primary and secondary sex characteristics, their genitals/anatomy, and the sociocultural context in which that child is reared. In those rare instances in which these dimensions are not in alignment, we witness an experience of gender identity conflict that can range from mild to quite severe.

> The average male fits in without difficulty, the atypical one who will exhibit signs of gender identity dysphoria, for instance, does not see himself as *same* or similar to others of his gender. He sees himself as *different* in likes and dislikes, preferences and attitudes but basically in terms of identity. There will be a period of confusion during which the child thinks something like *Mommy and*

Daddy call me boy, and yet I am not at all like any of the others that I know who are called "boy." While the only other category the child knows is *girl*, he develops the thought that he might be or should be one of those. Initially that thought is too great a concept leap to be easily accepted and the child struggles in an attempt to reconcile these awkward feelings. The boy might actually imagine he is, if not really a boy than possibly an *it*, an alien of some sort or a freak of nature. Eventually he might come to believe, since he knows of no other options, that he *is* a girl or should be one. And with a child's way of believing in Santa Claus or the Tooth Fairy he can come to expect he will grow up to be a woman. With experience and the realization that this won't happen of its own accord the maturing child may begin to seek ways to effect the desired change. A female can experience an opposite scenario.[37]

What is attractive about the brain-sex theory and various theories associated with it is that it attempts to offer a unifying theory of gender identity concerns in a way that is supported (according to proponents) by research.

Limitations. Several limitations of this research should be noted. These limitations include (1) small sample sizes, (2) post-mortem samples in which transsexual persons frequently used hormone therapy, and (3) emphasis on morphology rather than a range of other considerations.

In terms of sample sizes, the fact that gender incongruence and transsexuality are so rare makes it exceedingly difficult to obtain a large sample to conduct research. The most influential studies[38] in this area reported on findings of the neuroanatomical brain regions of six male-to-female transsexuals[39] and seven male-to-female transsexuals.[40]

Also, many studies involving transsexuals are based on post-mortem samples in which the person had been actively involved in cross-sex-typed behavior and had been utilizing feminizing hormone therapy in ways that may very well affect the regions under investigation. This is particularly true when referencing studies of the very neuroanatomical brain differences under discussion. As Zhou et al. acknowledged, "As all the transsexuals had been treated with oestrogens, the reduced size of the BSTc could possibly have been due to the presence of high levels of oestrogen in the blood,"[41] though they argue against that interpretation of their findings. What is needed, say critics, is research that utilizes a control group that would "exclude the possibility that the feminization of the BSTc in MtFs was due to hormone treatment, especially estrogen therapy, received for transsexualism."[42]

Some of the most influential studies today are based on observed differences in brain structure, whether that has to do with the number of cells present or the volume of cells in specific neuroanatomical regions of the brain.[43] These are essentially studies of morphology or brain structure, which is a rather limited way of conceptualizing the brain and potential observable differences. Beyond morphology or structure, there are also issues with brain activity, connectivity, load and efficiency that often go overlooked in a nearly exclusive focus on structure.[44]

Most proponents of a nature model for the etiology of gender identity concerns focus on the brain-sex theory and frequently point to the studies primarily of morphology: the size and shape of the brain region or cells. This points to one kind of sex difference, and it is real. But the study of morphology is only one of many possible ways to look at neurology. There is also activity—which area of the brain is more active in certain tasks? There is also connectivity and ways to assess whether there are gender differences in connectivity and what these mean. Then there is load, which is more like bandwidth or the thickness of the circuit. Finally, there is the question of efficiency. How efficient is the circuitry—is it highly mylenated, and are there significant differences in efficiency?

Also, when we consider research on identity, it is hard to imagine it being located in the hypothalamus. Self-concept is not rooted there but rather in the cortex.[45] Further, the whole idea of locating this sense of identity is problematic; as one expert in neurobiology shared, it is like finding a brain region for being a Democrat or a Republican; like finding a brain region for being an Asian American or being an animal-rights activist.[46]

It seems that any research on gender identity would also need to consider how the parietal lobe would be involved, as it is related to understanding one's body, as well as the frontal lobe for organizing self-awareness, let alone the temporal lobe for getting at sexuality. That there have been noted differences in the morphology of the brain in small samples is interesting, but it raises several other questions for future research.

There appears to be reason to at least take a step back and look at the larger picture here, to gain some perspective on what is being argued for and how best to conceptualize it.

I want to discuss a couple of alternatives to the brain-sex theory that have been a part of the larger discussion. They are Blanchard's typology of clinical

presentations and models based more on social learning as well as contributions from biology in the form of temperamental differences.

BLANCHARD'S TYPOLOGY

There is a group of researchers and clinicians who do not make strong claims
about etiology but rely on and advance a typology of transsexuality first introduced by Ray Blanchard. Blanchard suggested what to some are controversial[47] but distinct subtypes of transsexuals based on sexual attraction/ori-
entation, such as male-to-female androphilic type, which he contrasts with a
male-to-female autogynephilic type. The former is more of a "classic" presentation that is often referred to as the "homosexual" type because the person is
a biological male who is attracted to males. (The attraction is for a male who
is attracted to him as a woman, however.) These are "persons who typically
transition at a younger age, report more sexual attraction to and sexual experience with males, are unlikely to have married or to have been biologic
parents, and recall more childhood femininity."[48]

The autogynephilic type is described more like a fetish. In this case proponents assert that the biological male finds the idea of himself as a woman
sexually arousing. These are persons who "typically transition at an older age,
report more sexual attraction to and sexual experience with females, are more
likely to have married and to have become biologic parents, report more past
or current sexual arousal to cross-dressing or cross-gender fantasy, and recall
less childhood femininity."[49]

Another common presentation in Blanchard's typology would be the biological female who experiences herself as male (or female-to-male, FtM
type).[50] They are biologically/genetically female at birth but feel that they are
male in their gender identity. This person would not typically be attracted to
males and may have tried to enter into a same-sex relationship. However,
same-sex relationships often do not meet their needs for intimacy, as they
want to be close to a female who is drawn to them as a male.

Other clinical presentations based on sexual orientation include the bisexual type (with a history of sexual arousal to the same and opposite sex) and
the asexual/analloerotic type (with no or little arousal pattern).[51]

Many of the research studies that supporters of Blanchard's typology cite
were conducted between the mid-1980s and mid-1990s and include data on
many more transsexuals:

Blanchard's studies reported data on hundreds of transsexual males (that is, males who hoped to become or had become women), as well as other individuals who were male with respect to birth sex and did not desire sex reassignment surgery, but who sometimes presented themselves, or thought of themselves, as female. Participants in these studies were representative of gender patients in Canada, and were probably also quite similar to patients seen in the United States and Western Europe. Blanchard's goal was to make sense out of the diversity of patients that gender clinics saw.[52]

The main point in this review is that for many clinicians and theorists, the fact that there is an observable typology based upon sexual attraction/orientation suggests a more complicated pathway(s) for the etiology of gender identity concerns than is found in the brain-sex theory. Again, proponents of Blanchard's typology do not tend to take a position on etiology, but those who have advanced the brain-sex theory and others, particularly several transgender advocates, have been critical of Blanchard's typology and, in particular, autogynephilia.

Limitations. The primary concern I see raised by critics or opponents of Blanchard's typology is the distinction between the two types of male-to-female transsexuals: the androphilic type and the autogynephilic type. Recall that the androphilic MtF is believed to have a homosexual orientation, to have childhood experiences in common with what has been reported by adult homosexuals looking back on their childhood, and to express themselves in the more classic case of transsexualism (that is, "I am a woman trapped in the body of a man"). In contrast, the MtF autogynephilic type is described more like a fetish. It refers to a biological male who has a history of sexual arousal to the idea or fantasy of himself as female. It is this presentation that has been the primary concern. Most critics of Blanchard's typology tend to express support for the brain-sex theory and view Blanchard's typology as "unfalsifiable":

> It is unfalsifiable (note: any trans woman who reports that she doesn't fit the classifications is explained by the "theory" as being a "liar"). Furthermore, the scheme has no predictive capabilities. Thus it is thus untestable.[53]

Proponents of Blanchard's typology present this criticism as reflecting a kind of denial:

> Few nonhomosexual transsexuals publicly identify as autogynephilic, and most neither admit a history of sexual arousal to the idea of being a woman, nor

accept that such arousal was a motivating factor for their transsexualism. Indeed, although most public transsexual activists appear by their histories and presentations to be nonhomosexual MtF transsexuals, they have generally been hostile toward the idea that nonhomosexual transsexualism is associated with, and motivated by, autogynephilia.[54]

Here is the problem with "denial" at this point in the argument: ironically, by framing the criticism as denial we are left with support for the criticism that had been raised. That is, Blanchard's typology is at risk of being untestable if those who do not report a corresponding history are said to not be admitting the history, proponents of Blanchard's typology presuppose.

Also, it is unclear with Blanchard's typology whether the claim that cross-dressing is associated with sexual arousal (or had taken on a fetishistic quality) is referring to the present or the past in each case. It is possible that cross-dressing had at one time been associated with arousal or had taken on a fetishistic quality, perhaps during adolescence, but does not have that quality later in one's life.

In any case, it may be helpful to be aware of these controversies. Further, it should be noted that the *DSM-5* has moved away from specifiers that focus on sexual attraction or orientation.[55] The current preference is to discuss early and late onset Gender Dysphoria, which I will cover later.

MULTIFACTORIAL MODELS WITH AN EMPHASIS ON PSYCHOSOCIAL FACTORS

The other major explanatory framework comes from those who do advance multifactorial models that give greater weight to early psychosocial factors in childhood. Proponents begin with the assumption that the psychosocial environment is important. That is, basic concepts from cognitive theory and social learning theory are in play simply in the formation of one's gender identity. These are concepts that go back to Stoller[56] and Kohlberg[57] and of one's "core gender identity" or "fundamental sense of belonging to one sex."[58] That is, there is a cognitive process by which a child comes to know and understand his or her sense of gender and associated behaviors. There is a role that parenting and observational learning plays in terms of what is witnessed, modeled, and reinforced by parents, a broader family and kinship network, and one's peer group.

Meyer-Bahlburg[59] identifies several risk factors thought to be associated with the development of gender dysphoria. In addition to the prenatal sex hormone considerations associated with the brain-sex theory, these include (for biological males who are gender dysphoric) feminine appearance, inhibited/shy temperament, separation anxiety, late in birth order, sensory reactivity and sexual abuse. Also, associated risk factors related to parents include preference for a girl, parental indifference to cross-gender behavior, reinforcing cross-gender behavior, encouragement of "extreme physical closeness with boys," insufficient adult male role models and parental psychiatric issues.[60]

Veale and colleagues[61] review numerous studies on family and rearing environment and related considerations. Parental factors cited in the literature include less warm/emotionally distant fathers (although some studies do not show this difference), parental wishes for a girl (among MtF transsexual persons) and increased maternal involvement and parental support for gender variant behavior.[62] Higher reports of emotional, physical and sexual abuse have also been documented among gender-variant persons.[63]

These findings are primarily correlational. An experience or a quality may frequently occur with the phenomenon. For example, "Increased insecure attachment has been noted in boys" who are gender dysphoric.[64] So this different attachment pattern has been associated with gender dysphoria in boys. We would be speculating at causation (due to the design of the research), but is it possible that it is one of several considerations that contribute to gender dysphoria? It is also possible that gender dysphoria can contribute to difficulties with attachment.

Peer group interactions have also been noted by those who look at psychosocial influences on gender dysphoria. For example, boys who are gender dysphoric demonstrate "preferential adoption of cross-gender pretend play, and cross-dressing. Fear and avoidance of other boys can be striking. . . . A likely consequence of their preference for girl playmates is the continuous rehearsal of female role skills and habits, and a lack of development of male role skills and habits. The avoidance of contact with boys also implies a lack of peer group reinforcement for male-typical behavior; such peer-group reinforcement has been documented from middle preschool age on."[65]

But does that mean that nurture plays a role in gender dysphoria? In their review of this literature, Cohen-Kettenis and Gooren[66] identify the potential for a pathway to exist related to parental psychopathology and gender identity concerns, but they are correct in noting that those correlations should not be taken as causal, and that there are different explanations that could account for higher levels of psychopathology in parents who are coming to see a specialist in gender identity. What Cohen-Kettenis and Gooren did not see was much evidence that gender dysphoria is the result of a failure to identify with the same-sex parent.

Zucker and Bradley[67] proposed a theory that gender dysphoria may result from children who are more anxious and sensitive to others and who have a different response to tensions in the marriage or conflicts surrounding gender, as well as possible psychopathology on the part of their parents. Zucker has elsewhere discussed whether parents are preoccupied or otherwise distracted and unable to respond to or shape gender expressions.

Proponents of psychosocial models that look at the relative weight of psychosocial factors are not saying that these are the exclusive cause but rather that there are multiple factors that may make a contribution:

> A multifactorial model of gender development can take into account biological predisposing factors, precipitating factors, and perpetuating (maintenance) factors. Because so much is still not even known about normative gender development, . . . clinicians, patients, and their families vary in how much weight (or variance) each of these factors is given. At one extreme, some would argue that biological factors account for the bulk of the variance; at the other extreme, some would argue that psychosocial factors are most influential. . . . the propensity for practicing clinicians (and clients) to utilize dichotomous "either/or" paradigms in conceptualization is a common problem that should be avoided.[68]

Limitations. The limitations here are that many of the studies are correlational in design, so that they suggest a relationship between gender identity conflicts and other psychosocial considerations. However, it is often unclear which is the cause. For example, if a person was looking into parent-child relationships, we have to ask the question, does the parent's reaction, for example, come in response to gender atypicality, or does the gender atypicality elicit a specific parental response?

In the cases I have seen of young children, I have been impressed by the salience of their presentation, of their gender atypicality and, in some cases, extreme gender incongruence at a rather young age. Anecdotally, while parental interactions may clearly reinforce or maintain certain expressions of gender identity, the expressions that seemed so salient at age four or five did not appear to me to be the result of the parental interactions, modeling or attachment but rather the cause of parental concern.

Reflections on etiology. As I look over the limitations to the existing research, as well as what we know and what we do not know about causation at this point, it seems wise to consider any model of causation with some humility, almost holding it in an open hand with an understanding that we may know more in the years to come that will help us understand this topic better than we do today. I am also impressed by the amount of hostility directed at adherents of specific theories. There is a need not only for good research in this area, but a kind of open discussion that is not reduced to personal, ad hominem attacks.

It seems warranted that whatever model we work from today, it would ideally reflect a weighted interaction among multiple contributing factors— contributions that come from both nature and nurture. The contributions could take many forms, some of which we have discussed, and, as I have suggested, they would be weighted differently for different people. There may also be other factors in play that we have yet to identify. An appropriate amount of humility can be found in saying, *We don't know what causes gender dysphoria.*

As we consider a weighted interactionist model of some kind, I am reminded of two important concepts: *equifinality* and *multifinality*. *Equifinality* says that there could be multiple pathways to the same outcome. It seems reasonable, given the range of experiences of gender identity concerns (that I believe reside along a continuum), that there are likely many possible pathways to the same outcome if that outcome is the umbrella term *transgender* or *gender incongruence* or *gender identity concerns.* The outcome of transsexuality as a most extreme experience of gender dysphoria may indeed best be explained by the brain-sex theory, but I would not want to hold that out as a unifying theory that has to explain all experiences of transsexuality.

Multifinality says that a group of people could have the same factors as part of their history but have different outcomes.[69] Not every child who experiences a push from nature will end up experiencing gender identity conflicts. It seems as though other variables need to be in the mix, and it is difficult to say with great confidence what those are.

Something like the brain-sex theory could be in play for some experiences of transsexuality. But what if the various factors were weighted differently for different people? Would we then be able to account for other experiences of gender identity concerns along a continuum? Would a broader model that allows for the possibility of the brain-sex theory but is not limited to it provide for a more nuanced understanding that helps us understand the heterogeneity of presentations?

I tend to agree that our current understanding of etiology simply does not provide us with an "empirically grounded detailed theory of the mechanisms and process of gender identity development."[70] This seems like a reasonable conclusion to draw at this time. It would be premature to stand behind any one model that then makes exclusive proclamations about the determinants of gender identity concerns. I suspect that a weighted interactionist model of etiology would consider contributions from both nature and nurture, from both biology and environment without giving too much weight at this point to any one unifying theory. This means not being sold on the brain-sex theory while simultaneously demonstrating an openness to the theory as more research in this area is provided.

It could be that for some people a very narrow window exists in which the causes of gender incongruence are largely biological as the brain-sex theory suggests, while for most other people who report gender identity concerns, experiences of gender identity conflicts come from other, more varied sources that are weighted differently for different people, thus contributing to the wide range of gender variant presentations. For less severe gender identity presentations, perhaps the biological contributions take the form of temperamental and personality differences or sensory reactivity, followed by environmental conditions and social learning, among other factors, including but not limited to parental preferences, indifferences, reinforcement and modeling.[71] For some people, the biological contributions could be weighted even more, perhaps even to the point suggested by the brain-sex theory.

Other factors may be difficult to identify as clearly from nature or from nurture; they interact. For example, a biological male who has a feminine appearance may have such an appearance due to nature, but the environment and how others interact with him may also make a significant contribution. Similarly, insecure attachment may come from contributions from nature but also from environment, as when a child experiences insecure attachment as a result of abuse.

CONCLUDING THOUGHTS

I have been told, "If you know one transgender person, you know one transgender person!" In other words, there are so many variations in experience and presentation that knowing one transgender person tells you very little about transgender persons as a group. That may be true. Important questions remain about etiology, and we have already established that the transgender umbrella is quite broad. I am not optimistic that one unifying theory will explain the myriad presentations that exist under that particular canopy.

What I have been able to conclude about etiology is exactly what I told Jeremy and recounted at the opening of this chapter: "I don't think you chose to experience gender dysphoria." At some point in my work with a person who experiences gender identity conflicts, I will ask something like this: "What would it mean for you to know?" In other words, "What is the significance to you personally of having a working theory of causation?" Part of what I am saying is this: "How would I know if you experienced gender dysphoria due to various contributions from nature or key events in your environment (nurture)?" I would not be able to be certain. Neither will the person who is navigating gender identity concerns. I keep in mind that most people do develop a kind of storyline for themselves for their experiences of gender dysphoria. We can discuss that storyline, as well as other possible narratives, without the clinician imposing one on the client. It can be a kind of personal, working hypothesis, and it may not be the same for the client and for the clinician.

Another question for reflection is this: What is volitional here? A person can choose whether to engage in cross-gender behavior (or, to a lesser extent and to remind us of the continuum, gender bending behaviors of one kind or another). The experience of true gender dysphoria, however, is not chosen, nor is it a sign of willful disobedience, personal sin or the sin of the parents as such.

What can be difficult to discern is what kind of gender identity conflict we are witnessing. With the many ways in which a person can experience gender identity concerns (organized by onset; organized by sexual orientation; organized by purpose of cross-dressing or meaning, or other factors), how does this person's cross-gender interests fit into a larger meaning-making structure for this person? We can distinguish between those who bend gender roles in dress as a way of forming a sense of distinct and countercultural identity from those who are expressing their sense of their "true" self from those who are managing a dysphoria they wish would abate. Along these lines, it seems different to think about cross-dressing for sexual arousal and cross-dressing to manage gender dysphoria. It seems different to think about cross-dressing behavior as performance (i.e., drag) and cross-dressing to express one's core sense of self.

When I think of also considering a Christian worldview, it is important to reflect on our integrated framework first discussed in chapter two. Recall that an integrated framework looks at the strengths of three existing frameworks: the *integrity* framework, the *disability* framework, and the *diversity* framework. The brain-sex theory and related models reflect more of a diversity framework in which gender identity issues are merely a reflection of variations in nature across the various factors that are involved. It could reflect a disability framework to some extent, but most adherents do not use language that would suggest that; perhaps some proponents of the brain-sex theory would consider a disability framework if the dysphoria were causing distress and disruption in various social roles.

Proponents of Blanchard's typology seem less certain of a causal pathway. I do hear more of a concern among some proponents of Blanchard's typology that gender dysphoria can function like a disability—again, insofar as the condition causes a person social distress and impairment. Zucker's view also seems concerned about the gender dysphoria in and of itself as a reflection of a disability of sorts as a person is longing for quite invasive interventions to express cross-gender identification and to resolve gender dysphoria.

An integrated framework would reflect some regard for all three of these explanatory frameworks. Let's at least begin here in our discussion of etiology.

The integrity framework reminds us that God had a purpose in creating humankind male and female. We take seriously our biological sex and our gendered selves and how our sex and gender are parts of how we experience ourselves and relate to one another. Experiences like gender dysphoria, while they might be considered variations along the lines suggested by brain-sex theory, also exist in the context of a fallen world. The integrated framework also reminds me that because we live in a fallen world, questions about etiology are essentially questions about specific ways in which the fall casts its shadow all around and through us—in this case how the fall touches sex and gender in unique and uncertain ways. Also, the integrity framework gives us pause when we might otherwise focus on celebrating a gender dysphoria as though it were an expression of diversity as such or using such experiences to deconstruct sex and gender as though biological sex was an arbitrary source of oppression.

A disability framework reminds us of the benefits seen in viewing gender identity concerns as morally neutral. Keep in mind that the person who is navigating these concerns has not chosen to experience dysphoria. The incongruence between their biological sex and their gender identity is, in and of itself, not an act of willful disobedience. When we consider how best to care for someone who is navigating gender identity concerns, we can respond with compassion, keeping in mind that the person we are meeting with will face some painful and unique challenges in managing their dysphoria, which we will discuss in greater detail in chapter six.

The diversity framework emphasizes the variation as a cause for identity and for recognition and celebration. The identity comes in being transgender or in adopting a cross-gender role through any number of ways of expressing one's true self. The recognition and celebration can come from many different theories of etiology, although I suspect many proponents of a diversity framework are less concerned with theories of etiology and might be more concerned if a theory were to be used to further marginalize or pathologize a people group. Those who adopt a diversity framework likely do not know a specific causal pathway, but they might adopt a brain-sex model insofar as it can register as a model of identity in keeping with essentialist assumptions that help a group's cause in the broader cultural discussion and popular perception of transgender persons. The diversity framework may bias us toward the brain-sex theory over the others, so we want to consider any theory of etiology with humility about what we know and do not know at this time.

How we provide services to someone and address fundamental issues of identity and community, however, should be informed by a nuanced understanding for how the existing diversity framework provides significant meaning and purpose that is often not found in the Christian community when it comes to the care and counsel of those who experience gender dysphoria.

4

Phenomenology and Prevalence

THE PHENOMENOLOGY AND PREVALENCE of gender incongruence are related in part because the range of gender variant expressions and identities makes finding accurate prevalence estimates a challenge. In some respects, prevalence estimates were relatively clearer under the prior designation of Gender Identity Disorder. The change to Gender Dysphoria broadened the definition and scope of what may count as a gender identity concern. Also, I use the phrase "relatively clearer" because there were problems obtaining prevalence estimates with Gender Identity Disorder, too, as I will discuss below. Also, there are cultural expressions that are more common, such as cross-dressing behaviors for sexual arousal or as a fetish and various gender "bending" behaviors that are not quite the same thing as gender incongruence.

It has been helpful to many people to think about gender identity issues along a continuum. Gender dysphoria has been defined as "unhappiness with one's given gender."[1] This is not just feeling unhappy with being either male or female; nor is it identifying advantages to being the other sex. It is a more substantive "unhappiness," if you will, and it is a substantive unhappiness that leads to distress.

We can distinguish experiences of gender dysphoria from the diagnosis of Gender Dysphoria. When mental health professionals consider a diagnosis of Gender Dysphoria (which I will capitalize for the sake of clarity), they are saying that this "unhappiness with one's given gender" has risen to the level of an enduring, significant cross-gender identification and personal distress or impairment in important areas of functioning, such as work or school.

Gender Dysphoria can be diagnosed in children, adolescents or adults as— in the language of one of the most widely read diagnostic manuals—a "marked incongruence between one's experienced/expressed gender and assigned gender, of at least 6 months' duration."[2]

GENDER DYSPHORIA IN CHILDREN

When Gender Dysphoria is diagnosed in children, six of eight other symptoms would be present, and one of those symptoms has to be the first one on the list ("A strong desire to be of the other gender or an insistence that one is the other gender"). Symptoms include:

- A strong desire to be of the other gender or an insistence that one is the other gender.

- In boys (assigned gender), a strong preference for cross-dressing or simulating female attire; or in girls (assigned gender), a strong preference for wearing only typical masculine clothing and a strong resistance to the wearing of typical feminine clothing.

- A strong preference for cross-gender roles in make-believe play or fantasy play.

- A strong preference for the toys, games, or activities stereotypically used or engaged in by the other gender.

- A strong preference for the playmates of the other gender.

- In boys (assigned gender), a strong rejection of typically masculine toys, games, and activities and a strong avoidance of rough-and-tumble play; or in girls (assigned gender), a strong rejection of typically feminine toys, games, and activities.

- A strong dislike of one's sexual anatomy.

- A strong desire for the primary and/or secondary sex characteristics that match one's experienced gender.[3]

These experiences in a child would also be distressing to the child or would be impairing in an important area of functioning, such as school.

My experience has been that many Christians respond negatively to the language of "assigned gender." As I will discuss below, Christians are not alone in expressing reservations about this change in language and conceptualization. This change in the *DSM-5* was meant to include those who are intersex, that is, those who have a condition that makes it difficult to identify their sexual anatomy at childbirth. In cases in which this occurs, the gender has often been assigned by the doctor or by the parents in consultation with a medical team and sometimes with disastrous results. The book *As Nature Made Him* documents the case of a baby boy who underwent a botched circumcision and who was raised as a girl at a time when some experts were quite confident that social learning could trump biology.[4] The boy, John, was actually unable to sustain an identity as a female (Joan) and transitioned to male in adolescence. Tragically, as an adult he took his own life.

When we think about "assigned gender," the phrase is meant to remind us of these kinds of intersex experiences—whether as a result of a mishap at the time of circumcision or a medical condition such as Androgen Insensitivity Syndrome. The point here is that this is probably not how most Christians think about being identified as a boy or girl at birth. Most parents do not think in terms of "assigned gender." Other phrases that are frequently used would be "natal gender," "birth sex" or "biological sex." A case could be made for each of these phrases, and professionals in the field demonstrate a preference for any one of these phrases today. The language is meant to communicate to the reader that in the experience of gender dysphoria there exists a contrast between that assigned/natal/birth/biological gender/sex and the child's "experienced" or "expressed" gender. It is that lack of congruence or correspondence that is part of what is being assessed.

The challenge that exists in making this kind of diagnosis in a child is distinguishing between experiences of gender atypicality, in which a child might behave outside of gender norms or stereotypes, and when a child truly expresses a kind of gender incongruence that warrants a diagnosis. In other words, many children may be "subthreshold," or below the threshold of a diagnosis.

Also, situation/context is critical. I have met with boys who have a sister near their age and only have girls in their immediate neighborhood. Their play is often with girls. This alone would not be considered a strong preference for playmates who are girls, so that has to be differentiated.

> *The mother of a six-year-old Caucasian boy calls for services. She reports concern about his mannerisms and voice inflection—that it is more effeminate—and she fears he will be teased in school. She has already had family members and people at the park comment on his mannerisms.*
>
> *The mother and father report that their son's cross-dressing started at age three and that he would also play dress up as a female at his friend's house. They noticed*

female gestures and mannerisms at age five (e.g., hand on hip, wrist). They indicated his play group was primarily females.

His parents confirmed that their son stated that he wished God had made him a girl. They reported consistent identification with his mother, stating that he wanted to be like her, and little identification with his father or older brother.

I have at times seen a lack of identification with the same gender parent among those children whose parents report a gender identity concern. Many boys who do not have a history of gender identity conflicts will identify with their father and name ways in which they are similar. If a boy sees his father come out of the shower, he might say, "Dad, you have a penis like I have a penis!" There is a sense in which he sees in his father aspects of himself, and vice versa.

Not only can that be absent in a child who experiences gender dysphoria, but the identification seems to be with the adult figure of the other sex. In the case above, I mentioned that the six-year-old tended to identify with his mother. What does that even mean? For this particular boy, he would grab a towel and wrap it around his head, letting the length of the towel go down his back. He would exclaim, "I have long hair just like you, Mom!" Or he would wrap a towel around his waist as though it was a skirt or a dress and say, "I have a dress on just like you, Mom."

Here is the challenge: many kids may do something like this, and they are not Gender Dysphoric in the diagnostic sense, and they might not be particularly gender dysphoric in the broader sense of the term. They are playing; they are finding ways to connect with their mom or dad. That is one reason why a diagnosis is not made without identifying several ways in which a child expresses symptoms of Gender Dysphoria.

This is probably the most difficult distinction to communicate to people who have not worked with children who meet criteria for Gender Dysphoria. They will say, "Every child I know plays like that from time to time. It's not that unusual." Yes and no. While not all children engage in cross-sex-typed play, some do, so from that standpoint, I agree with the idea that it is not that uncommon. Certainly a diagnosis should not be made on that fact alone. However, when a child is truly gender dysphoric, the play means something different to that child than to a child who is not diagnosed with Gender Dysphoria.

In a study of children who presented with Gender Dysphoria, Steensma et al.[5] distinguished between those children whose dysphoria persisted into adolescence and those children whose dysphoria resolved. A biological male whose gender dysphoria persisted shared the following: "I always played with girls' stuff and I dressed up as a girl. I sometimes borrowed my sister's dress and had a furry sheet, which I tied on my head, pretending I had long hair."[6] A biological female whose gender dysphoria persisted shared the following: "The girls played with Barbie dolls, wore dresses and they gossiped. I never gossiped. I usually decapitated Barbie dolls, when I got them, and threw them in the dustbin. I played soccer, wore blue jeans, and played with marbles. I played with the boys and I was always in the company of the other boys."[7]

Symptoms of gender dysphoria are not just seen in play, however. In particular, how a child responds to his or her primary and secondary sex characteristics are important considerations. In that same study of children whose gender dysphoria persisted or desisted, those who persisted in their gender dysphoria experienced a marked discomfort "by the fact that their bodies did not conform to their feelings"; regarding anatomy, "persisting girls reported primarily desiring a penis, the persisting boys in contrast wished to get rid of their penis."[8] A biological female whose gender dysphoria persisted shared, "When I was standing in front of the mirror I did not very much mind seeing my genitals, but it made me very sad that I did not have a penis."[9]

As I indicated above, other considerations include the desire for cross-gender roles in fantasy play, strong interest in the activities and games often associated with the other gender, and so on.

GENDER DYSPHORIA IN ADOLESCENTS AND ADULTS

The *DSM-5* brings adolescent and adult experiences together for diagnostic purposes. The diagnostic criteria are the same for adolescents and adults but different than the criteria for children. In adolescents and adults, at least two of six symptom presentations would be evident, including:

- A marked incongruence between one's experienced/expressed gender and primary and/or secondary sex characteristics (or in young adolescents, the anticipated secondary sex characteristics).

- A strong desire to be rid of one's primary and/or secondary sex characteristics because of a marked incongruence with one's experienced/expressed gender (or in young adolescents, a desire to prevent the development of the anticipated secondary sex characteristics).

- A strong desire for the primary and/or secondary sex characteristics of the other gender.

- A strong desire to be the other gender (or some alternative gender different from one's assigned gender).

- A strong desire to be treated as the other gender (or some alternative gender different from one's assigned gender).

- A strong conviction that one has the typical feelings and reactions of the other gender (or some alternative gender different from one's assigned gender).[10]

Clinicians who work with a person who may meet criteria for Gender Dysphoria are also to note whether a person has an intersex condition. Recall from chapter one that an intersex condition is one in which at birth an infant was unable to be identified as male or female because of ambiguous genitalia. The ambiguous presentation may be due to any number of rare variations that can occur at the level of the chromosomes or gonads. There is also cultural momentum in some nations toward offering those with an intersex condition the option of identifying as either intersex or "X" as an alternative to the male-female binary.[11]

One of the benefits in meeting with an adolescent or adult is that now the person is older and able to more clearly articulate their experience with gender dysphoria. They may request hormonal treatment, surgery or find other ways to change how they appear to others. The challenges that arise, in my view, have to do with determining when an adolescent's experiences of gender dysphoria rise to the level of a diagnosis of Gender Dysphoria, when co-occurring issues are present and more salient (e.g., an anxiety disorder), and when family dynamics are such that an adolescent does not receive sufficient empathy and support to even come to an understanding of how to proceed and what options may lay before them.

A Christian couple came to therapy with their sixteen-year-old son. They state that he believed he was a girl, and that they were in conflict about how to relate and where to go from here. They expressed a preference that we refer to their son by his birth name, which was Colton. However, Colton preferred a different name, Caitlyn, but would still respond to his given name. Colton was visibly anxious and, after further assessment, met criteria for an anxiety disorder that kept him homebound from school. He expressed an interest in transitioning to female through hormonal treatment and sex-reassignment surgery. We discussed his options at this point and the current standards of care and what it would mean to wait until he was an adult at which time he could receive a referral to a specialty clinic. Of immediate concern, however, was his anxiety disorder and the effects of his anxiety on social and educational functioning. He was initially unwilling to talk about his anxiety and was convinced that it was due exclusively to his gender dysphoria, which he wanted to resolve through transition as soon as possible.

In adolescence those whose gender dysphoria persisted tended to want to express their gender identity, whether feminine (if a biological male) or masculine (if a biological female). That would be via dress, name/identification or behavior.[12] One biological male whose gender dyphoria persisted shared the following:

When I became older, I felt more and more uncomfortable when I had to change clothes in the company of the other boys in gym class. When we went to camp with school I desperately wanted to sleep together with the girls, but I was not allowed to. That was a difficult confrontation. I became more and more aware of how different I was from the other boys.[13]

One biological female who attempted to live in a female role despite significant gender dysphoria shared:

To prevent being bullied at my new high school, my mom advised me to wear girls' clothes and stimulated me to let my hair grow. In a way, I hoped and expected that my feeling of being a boy would change and that I would start to feel more like a girl. But from the day I went to my new school, I constantly questioned this whole plan. I was totally not interested in the things the girls were talking about, and felt very uneasy. I felt more and more unhappy with the role I was living in. I wanted to be with the other boys and talk about soccer. I wanted to be one of them.[14]

In any of these cases—whether a child, adolescent or adult presentation—what I want to be clear about is this: a person could have gender identity questions or concerns or experience gender dysphoria and not meet criteria for the diagnosis of Gender Dysphoria in the official diagnostic manual. Put differently, gender dysphoria can be experienced subthreshold and, as Zucker[15] observes, most children or adolescents who are subthreshold may have met criteria for Gender Dysphoria at a younger age with the movement from threshold to subthreshold being the result of efforts to intervene

(whether these are formal or informal). Indeed, most children who meet criteria for Gender Dysphoria do not continue to meet criteria as they grow up
and enter adolescence. According to the *DSM-5*, Gender Dysphoria persists
from childhood to adolescence in only 2.2 to 30 percent of biological males
and 12 to 50 percent of biological females.[16] Granted, that is a significant range,
and more consistent figures would help us understand the likelihood of per-
sistence (as well as possibly predicting variables), but for our purposes, we can
at least acknowledge that in most cases Gender Dysphoria desists over time
as children enter into adolescence.

Those who meet the threshold for Gender Dysphoria tend to display "significantly more cross-gender behavior or less same-gender behavior" than
those who are subthreshold.[17] Those who are subthreshold are still gender
nonconforming but essentially less so.

PREVALENCE

It is hard to get exact figures on how many people's symptoms rise to the level
of a diagnosable Gender Dysphoria (or, formerly, Gender Identity Disorder),
let alone experiences of gender dysphoria along a continuum. Most of the
research conducted to date was of Gender Identity Disorder, the language and
category used in the previous publication on mental health concerns. It is
relatively rare for someone to experience gender dysphoria to the extent that
we would diagnose that person with Gender Dysphoria, but because it resides
on a continuum, any estimates here are likely low when we think of children,
adolescents, and adults who experience gender dysphoria somewhere along
the continuum but likely do not meet criteria for the formal diagnosis as such
and are not going to a specialty clinic.[18]

The *DSM-5* estimates that between 0.005 percent to 0.014 percent of adult
males and 0.002 percent to 0.003 percent of adult females have Gender Dysphoria.[19] These estimates are based on people seeking out specialty clinics for
treatment. This is unlikely an accurate picture of gender dysphoria along a continuum. Findings from other studies put the prevalence estimates in ranges
from 1 in 10,000 to 1 in 13,000 males and 1 in 20,000 to 1 in 34,000 females.[20]

Identifying oneself as transgender is much more common. There is not a
lot of research on this, as most studies have not provided the option of transgender in the demographics section until relatively recently. Be that as it may,
between 1 in 215 and 1 in 300 people identified themselves as transgender in

two probability samples.[21] Because *transgender* is an umbrella term that encompasses many experiences of gender variance, experts[22] doubt whether these respondents would meet criteria for Gender Dysphoria, though many may experience some degree of gender dysphoria along a continuum.

Gender Dysphoria as a diagnosis and the broader experience of gender dysphoria along a continuum appears to be more common among males than females, with a ratio of at least 3:1. Zucker has put that ratio as high as 5:1 in terms of referrals to specialty clinics, and he has suggested that it may be due to a more narrow set of cultural expectations for boys to display acceptable masculine behaviors and mannerisms than girls. Think about it this way: even in the English language, we have a neutral word for a girl who demonstrates more masculine interests (i.e., she is tomboyish, which is not a derogatory statement), but we do not have a neutral word for a boy who demonstrates feminine interests. The language used in the 1970s was "sissy" or "sissy-boy syndrome," which has been discarded for obvious reasons. Language matters, as it reflects our assumptions of what is normal, what is acceptable and what is of concern.

Zucker[23] identified several criticisms of the former diagnosis of Gender Identity Disorder that in many ways continue to apply to the current diagnosis of Gender Dysphoria. These include that Gender Dysphoria is a normal variation in experiences of gender identity; that the distress associated with Gender Dysphoria is not inherent to the condition but a reflection of societal rejection; and that the diagnosis is a way to surreptitiously prevent homosexuality. There are debates about what constitutes a mental disorder that are beyond the scope of this chapter,[24] but I appreciate Zucker's observation about where the trajectory of Gender Dysphoria takes a person:

> It is difficult to argue that cross-gender feelings and behaviors simply constitute a normative variation or do not constitute an example of impairment if one considers the developmental adolescent or adult "end state," . . . i.e., the strong desire to align the body via contrasex hormones and sex-reassignment surgery. . . . The required physical interventions are simply too radical to be thought of otherwise.[25]

What are we to make of the distress? Is the distress a person's subjective reaction to cross-gender identification? Is it the subjective response to the incongruence? Or is it that but also the cross-gender identification in and of itself? For some experts in this area, the cross-identification is itself a reflection of distress. For example, Zucker goes on to say that the decision to live in a "cross-gendered role" reflects an "in-the-person distress regarding the disjunction between somatic sex and felt psychological gender."[26] It does not do justice to the phenomenon to say that the dysphoria is simply the result of rejection from others. I would concur with Zucker that the desire to be the other sex is itself a reflection of distress, a conflict that resides within between one's somatic or phenomenal self and one's psychological or emotional experience of oneself *vis-a-vis* one's gender identity.

A challenge that arises is that not all gender nonconformity rises to the level of this cross-gender identification. Remember that this is an extreme and rare form of cross-gender identification that we now refer to as Gender Dysphoria. But gender dysphoria (in a broader sense that is subthreshold) can exist and may not be experienced subjectively by the person in question as distressing, and may very well not rise to the level of true distress in and of itself. This is certainly a complex and complicated area for reflection and consideration.

So there is wisdom in viewing gender dysphoria broadly or along a continuum, to think more broadly than just those who meet criteria for a formal diagnosis of Gender Dysphoria or who are pursuing sex-reassignment surgery.[27] Certainly gender dysphoria can exist without the desire for hormonal treatment or surgery.

As we bring this chapter to a close, I also want to revisit the use of the term *transgender*. Recall that in chapter one we introduced how *transgender* is an umbrella term for the many ways in which people might experience the gender identity that is different from those in the majority (who experience a sense of congruence between their gender identity and biological sex). *Transgender* as an umbrella terms extends, too, beyond just the experience of gender identity but also to its presentation or expression (i.e., how it is lived out).

So a person may identify as transgender and be a cross-dresser or someone who dons the clothing of the other gender. We can think of the various aspects involved in cross-dressing across the purpose, extent and locale. The purposes of cross-dressing can vary widely. A person could identify as male in nearly all social settings but cross-dress in a way that expresses another aspect of his gender identity (more for identity validation or expression). Or a person could cross-dress for primarily sexual reasons (sexual arousal). A person could cross-dress as a way of managing gender dysphoria—that is, when the person cross-dresses, the dysphoria he feels lessens to some extent or becomes more manageable. Drag queens and drag kings cross-dress. They perform in a theatrical setting and in a theatrical manner. That can be as a means of expression or as a way to feel arousal. As I have shared previously, they may not experience gender dysphoria or identify as transgender, and some within the transgender community would not see those who perform drag as transgender as such.

Table 4.1. Facets of Cross-Dressing: Purpose, Extent, Locale

Purpose	Expression	Management	Arousal
Extent	Underwear	Outerwear	Outerwear/makeup/hair
Locale	At home/private	Public/out of the area	Public/local area

So a person could cross-dress but not experience gender dysphoria; they might cross-dress because the act of cross-dressing is itself sexually arousing. Kimber[28] offers a helpful, educated guess as to what the ratio would be of those who cross-dress in relation to those who eventually seek hormonal treatment and sex-reassignment surgery. Based on these calculations, most cross-dressers either only wear underwear of the other's sex (about 68% of all who cross-dress) or only wear other sex clothing at home (21%), in contrast to those who range from occasionally cross-dressing when they are out all the way to the person who transitions through hormonal treatment and sex-reassignment surgery. Essentially, Kinder's estimate is that only one out of three hundred persons who already cross-dresses would make that kind of transition.

The extent of cross-dressing also varies considerably. One person could cross-dress by only wearing undergarments or even a symbolic/meaningful necklace. This can range from something quite unnoticeable to donning an entire outfit that also includes make-up and hairstyle or wig.

In terms of locale, cross-dressing can occur in private or in public. It can be done at home and essentially in private (use of underwear) or at home and in public (cross-dressing in front of one's family). Or cross-dressing could be done in a public way but out of the person's local community, as when a person travels and cross-dresses primarily in that other setting. Cross-dressing could also be done in one's local community in a public way.

BLANCHARD'S TYPOLOGY

When we consider gender dysphoria in adulthood, there are again some controversies about how to conceptualize various presentations. One typology suggests three common presentations: (1) Female-to-Male Gender Dysphoria; (2) Male-to-Female Gender Dysphoria (Androphilic Type) and (3) Male-to-Female Gender Dysphoria (Autogynephilic Type).[29]

Those who are biologically/genetically female at birth but feel that they are male in their gender identity (referred to as Female-to-Male Gender Dysphoric or FtM) typically have long identified as masculine and did not want to be dressed in female attire. They frequently spoke of wanting to be a boy (or that they were a boy), and they had a negative response to the changes their body went through at puberty. Blanchard offers the following description:

> Puberty usually brings great emotional turmoil to homosexual female gender dysphorics. They hate their menses, which privately remind them that their bodies are female, and their developing breasts, which proclaim the same fact to the outside world. The awakening of sexual interest in other females brings a new poignancy to their longing for male genitals; the beginnings of dating and going steady among their adolescent peers contrast their frustrated dreams of love with the common reality of others.[30]

A female-to-male client has not typically been attracted to males; further, they may have tried same-sex because they feel male inside. However, these relationships are not typically satisfying to them. What they are seeking is for a female to be attracted to them as a male.

Clients who are biologically/genetically male at birth but feel that they are female in their gender identity (referred to as Male-to-Female Gender Dysphoric or MtF) have two common presentations: Androphilic Type and Autogynephilic Type. A person who presents as Male-to-Female Androphilic Type is more of the direct parallel to the female-to-male discussed above. The androphilic person was viewed as more effeminate from a young age. As a boy, he often avoided physical rough play and may have shown a preference to dress in female attire, to take on a female persona in play/games, and to prefer being called a female name.[31] This boy would often have a strong bond with his mother. The act of cross-dressing is not thought to be sexually arousing (in contrast to the autogynephilic type, which I describe below). If he tries romantic relationships it might be with another male, but same-sex relationships are not typically emotionally satisfying because he is looking for a male who is attracted to him as a female. As Blanchard puts it:

> Homosexual gender dysphorics maintain that their sexual interest in other men

is actually heterosexual, because "inside" they really are women. They also prefer partners who are heterosexual—who claim to be so—and who concur with the transsexual's self-evaluation that he is "really" a woman. Transsexuals, therefore, reject lovers who show an interest in their male genitals, not only because they hate their genitals to be touched in the first place, but also because they conclude (probably correctly) that these men are homosexual.[32]

The person presenting as Male-to-Female Autogynephilic Type is sometimes referred to as expressing the heterosexual or transvestic form because in some descriptions it appears as a kind of fetish. According to Blanchard,[33] this person's early history is not unlike that of others who present with tranvestism in that most are interested in gender typical male activities as boys; most experience some arousal when cross-dressing; they tend to work in more male-dominated professions/occupations, and so on. Richard Carroll[34] also offers that, as a child, the heterosexual type presentation may have been more masculine. He would typically have dressed in his mother's (or sister's) clothing prior to puberty and found that arousing. He would typically report being attracted to females and often puts himself in almost hyper-masculine roles, such as weightlifting, law enforcement or the military. He is more likely to marry someone of the opposite sex. Over time, he may feel the need to transition to female, and this is considered the most common presentation among biological males seeking hormonal treatment and sex-reassignment surgery. According to proponents of this distinction, the psychology of male-to-female autogynephilia appears to be arousal at the thought/fantasy of oneself as female, which is where the fetish quality comes to the foreground. This client would likely be sexually attracted to women and would also fantasize/imagine himself as female. Carroll explains autogynephilia: "The term refers to the experience of sexual arousal (philia) to the fantasy of oneself (auto) as being a female (gyne)."[35]

Lawrence, in one of the most complete resources comprised of the personal narratives of autogynephilic individuals, refers to their experiences as "men trapped in men's bodies,"[36] by which she means to contrast their experience with the male-to-female androphilic presentation of being a "woman trapped in a man's body." The experience of the autogynephilic individual does appear to reflect "a sexual desire that accompanies the desire to be female."[37]

Blanchard notes that for the male-to-female autogynephilic person (heterosexual or transvestic form), interest in cross-dressing often creates a conflict:

> Many have realistic fears about their ability to "pass" as women; others fear having their anomaly discovered by their families, friends, or colleagues at work. A common compromise is going out in women's attire for a solitary walk or drive, usually late at night when there are few people around. . . .
>
> Whether or not he overcomes his fear of going in public cross-dressed, the heterosexual gender dysphoric is increasingly confronted with another, more serious problem: the frustrating conflict between his desire to live as a woman and his reluctance to abandon his wife, children, or career. This is the point at which these patients typically present for treatment.[38]

Blanchard hypothesized that there may be different manifestations of autogynephilic interests (behaviors and fantasies): "*transvestic* (involving wearing women's apparel), *anatomic* (involving possessing female anatomic features), *physiologic* (involving having female physiologic functions), and *behavioral* (involving engaging in stereotypically feminine behavior)."[39]

Blanchard describes other clinical presentations of gender dysphoria, such as the bisexual gender dysphoric type (with a history of sexual arousal to the same and opposite sex) and the asexual/analloerotic type (with no or little arousal pattern).[40] But these appear less frequently than the more common presentations noted above.

EARLY AND LATE ONSET

I mentioned earlier that the *DSM-5* has moved away from specifiers that focus on attraction or orientation, which are key aspects of Blanchard's typology. Rather, the *DSM-5* includes early and late onset as specifiers. These are generally thought to apply in particular to male-to-female transgender persons. In a helpful summary of the clinical evidence collected to date, Zucker and Brown describe the more common experiences and concerns of early-onset male-to-female transgender persons:

> Early-onset [male-to-female transgender persons] often recount significant histories of social exclusion and harassment over long periods of time. They tend to have high degrees of social anxiety and may be less socially skilled on account of having lesser practice within peer networks. Some of this may be resolved through transition, but there is typically quite a bit of residual work regarding grieving the experiences they have missed out on, low self-esteem, and the anxiety of being discovered as trans, as early transitioners often choose

to live "stealth" (i.e., not disclose their transition history to most others). If their families are not supportive, this group is much more vulnerable to home-lessness, to using substances to cope, and/or to survival sex work.[41]

Zucker and Brown also offer a helpful description of male-to-female trans-gender persons who experience late-onset gender dysphoria:

> Late-onset [male-to-female transgender persons] have mostly grown up with fairly traditional masculine childhoods and the psychological steadiness and resilience that acceptance and "fitting in" (at least from the outside) can bring. Contemplating transition is often frightening, as the stripping of privilege and potential losses in relationship and employment can be sudden and staggering. If they lose core parts of their lives, which many do, there may also not be an easy transition into new communities or employment opportunities. Many could be helped with great work and/or by finding new supports or activities.[42]

When we think of time of onset as a key distinction between how people might experience and present with gender identity concerns, we can distin-guish between early onset and late onset. Early onset is the more common presentation, though it is likely to diminish or resolve in most people who experience it.

CONCLUDING THOUGHTS

As I bring this chapter to a close, we should recognize that gender dysphoria that rises to the level of a diagnosable disorder (Gender Dysphoria) is quite rare. People may experience gender dysphoria or a kind of gender incon-gruence along a continuum, and the prevalence estimates likely rise when we start discussing the experience along these lines. Any continuum might in-clude gender-bending behaviors among adolescents and young adults, which may or may not reflect gender dysphoria, as well as gender variant expressions and identities and the range of experiences under the transgender umbrella, such as persons who identify as genderfluid, genderqueer, cross-dressers, drag kings and queens, transvestites, and intersex. As I noted in chapter one, not everyone who is in each of these categories (e.g., drag king) would consider themselves transgender, and not all transgender persons would count each of these categories of people as belonging under the transgender umbrella. Cer-tainly not all experience gender dysphoria. However, as we think about prev-alence estimates, recent probability studies suggest prevalence is much higher when people are given the option of selecting "transgender" as an identifier than when we base prevalence on those who are formally diagnosed with Gender Dysphoria or who present at specialty clinics.

Also, it should not be underestimated that gender dysphoria, insofar as it may be experienced to varying degrees by many different kinds of people who fall under the transgender umbrella, represents an issue within our culture that is hugely symbolic. In the context of the social and cultural discussions and debates (and political wars) surrounding sex and gender and ethics, it represents to some an opportunity to challenge structures of authority that they have experienced as oppressive. To others it represents an effort to deconstruct meaningful designations of sex and gender. To still others it may represent great pain and hardship that seem to offer few satisfying pathways to resolution.

The Christian community faces a unique challenge in rising above the culture wars and these symbolic dimensions as we think about how to engage both the broader culture and the individual who is navigating gender identity questions. There remains the theological challenge associated with thinking clearly about sex and gender, debates about essentialism and social constructivism, and theological anthropology and ethics. There also remains the pastoral challenge of how to translate that theological work into the practical necessities and pastoral accommodations associated with compassionate care for the persons who are navigating gender incongruence in their lives.

5

Prevention and Treatment
of Gender Dysphoria

"What can we do?" asked the mother of a seven-year-old boy. She looked up and caught my eye. "What should we do? Just last week a woman at the park said something. I couldn't believe she had the nerve, but she did. I'm worried about him; I'm afraid that kids at school might do worse. There have been a few things said, at least he has hinted at a couple of things. But that could get worse. How they might tease him . . . I don't know. . . ." The mother went on to describe her son's effeminate behavior and mannerisms, as well as how his voice inflection seemed more like that of a girl's. She spoke of his tendency to pretend he had long hair and declare, "Mom, I have long hair like you have long hair!" She shared that just this past weekend, he grabbed a towel and put it around his waist and said, "Look, Mom, I'm wearing a dress just like you!" And he would often put on her heeled shoes and walk around in them.

This was a challenging situation for the parents. They were unsure how to respond to their son. They did not know if this was a phase he was going through, although they hoped it was just that. They did not know if it was a sign that he was going to be gay. They did not know what gender incongruence or gender dysphoria was, so that was not even on their radar.

This chapter looks at ways in which professionals respond to gender dysphoria in childhood, adolescence and adulthood. The responses to childhood experiences of gender dysphoria are controversial and differ significantly from responses to adolescent and adult experiences of gender dysphoria.

IN CHILDHOOD

Most cases of gender incongruence in childhood resolve by the time the child reaches adolescence or adulthood. That many desist in their experience of gender incongruence and dysphoria has been noted in recent research.[1] It is also possible that gender incongruence is suppressed so that it is not seen or, in the case of a friend, repressed (outside of conscious awareness) and then comes back to his awareness several years into his marriage.

When we consider the possibility of gender dysphoria desisting, the debates center on whether the resolution occurs "naturally," if you will, or if therapy can be provided to facilitate a reduction in gender incongruence and dysphoria. The most vocal critics of such practices demean it (and the professionals who provide it) as a version of conversion therapy, likening it to attempts to change sexual orientation. Outspoken critics of conversion or reorientation therapy often liken it to bleaching an African American's skin in response to his or her own self-hatred and racial stigma.

Ideally these clinical issues will be answered through well-designed research studies of the likelihood of various interventions producing favorable results. Research, of course, provides us with information on what we are able to do; it does not answer questions about what we ought to do. That is a question for philosophical ethics and theology.

As we look at responding to childhood experiences of gender dysphoria, the four options here for discussion are

1. resolution of gender dysphoria through intervention to decrease cross-gender identification

2. watchful waiting

3. facilitation of the gender identity of the preferred sex in anticipation of an adult identification

4. intervention to block hormones until a child (now a teen) can decide about gender identity in later adolescence

The literature often distinguishes three options by essentially combining psychosocial facilitation of cross-sex identification with movement toward puberty suppression.[2] However, I see these as two similar but different approaches. Although they share a common trajectory (toward facilitating cross-gender identification, i.e., the gender identity of the preferred sex), it should be noted that psychosocial facilitation can take place without the use of puberty suppressing hormones.

Table 5.1. Approaches to Childhood Experiences of Gender Dysphoria

Decrease Cross-Gender Identification	Watchful Waiting	Psychosocial Facilitation	Puberty Suppression
Emphasis on resolution of Gender Dysphoria by decreasing cross-gender behaviors and identification.	Take a neutral approach that allows for cross-gender dress and role adaption while avoiding reinforcement.	Facilitating expression of a gender role that reflects a child's gender identity.	Use of puberty-suppressing hormones to delay puberty until an adolescent can decide about gender identity.

Decrease cross-gender behavior/identification. Those who provide interventions to resolve gender dysphoria by decreasing cross-gender behavior/ identification frame their work as facilitating desisting what they believe will occur in most cases anyway.[3] Proponents of early intervention also consider whether those whose gender dysphoria persists and those whose desists represent two different conditions. It is unclear whether those are two different issues at present, but perhaps future research will answer that question or at least provide greater insight. Also, proponents note that the known emotional and social correlates of gender incongruence—issues like family and peer conflict and ostracism, as well as depression, anxiety, school aversion and school drop-out—provide a rationale for intervention:

> These sequelae . . . are our primary reason for its treatment. We expect that we can diminish these problems if we are able to speed up the fading of cross-gender identity which will typically happen in any case.[4]

There are, generally speaking, two broad approaches—behavioral and psychodynamic—with the more recent proposal for a third treatment approach. Behavioral therapy encourages the same-sex parent (or grandparent or mentor) to spend more time and share positive play experiences with their child while also avoiding criticism of the child. The parents are coached to essentially ignore cross-sex-typed behavior if at all possible and identify strategies to redirect the child to behaviors that reflect more that child's gender.[5] In following an operant conditioning approach, parents praise the child for any gender-appropriate activities or play.

Psychodynamic approaches (psychoanalysis, psychotherapy, psychoanalytic psychotherapy) based on object relations, self psychology and other conceptualizations take a developmental perspective, explore identification with the same and opposite sex, and intervene more "within" the child (than through the environment).[6]

Those who provide similar services today combine some of the approaches presented above into a hybrid or "third way" model.[7] They extend the treatment beyond simple behavioral reinforcement by providing therapy to address a child's gender incongruence and identity from the "inside out," while also setting limits and providing education to address gender identity from the "outside in."[8] Parents are also provided assistance in identifying activities that facilitate a same-gender identification, and there is typically a significant increase in time spent with same-sex peers (milieu protocol) that has been shown in research to be associated with "more typical sex-differentiated behavior."[9]

As I mentioned, one rationale for such intervention is the social climate and peer group disapproval that is associated with gender variant identity and behavior in elementary, middle and high school years.[10] Another is that with intervention there does seem to be a decrease in the number of people who persist in their gender incongruence into adolescence and adulthood.[11]

Meyer-Bahlburg[12] offers a protocol for intervention to facilitate the resolution of gender dysphoria among biological males. That protocol focuses on the following:

- Fostering positive relationship with one's father or male caregiver or role model
- Fostering positive relationships with one's male peers
- Fostering gender-typical habits and skills
- Facilitating male peer group interactions
- Facilitating positive feelings about being male

This kind of protocol is rather eclectic, with aspects of social learning theory and behavioral and milieu therapy approaches. To reduce stigmatization, the protocol focuses on services to the parents who work with the child rather than work directly with the child. Other approaches include direct therapy with the child as well as work with parents and the school system.

There has been research conducted on outcomes with Gender Dysphoric children when intervention is in place to prevent dysphoria from continuing into adolescence and adulthood. For example, a National Public Radio report on the topic cited the Portman Clinic's treatment of 124 children since 1989.[13] The approach taken at the Portman Clinic is to have children live in a way that is consistent with their birth sex. It was reported that 80 percent of the children chose later as adults to maintain a gender identity consistent with their birth sex.

The main controversy in intervening to prevent gender dysphoria has to do with a connection between gender dysphoria in childhood and adult homosexuality. Most children who are gender dysphoric find that the dysphoria resolves before adolescence. The *DSM-5* offers ranges for persisting at between 2.2 percent and 30 percent of gender dysphoric biological males and at 12 percent and 50 percent of gender dysphoric biological females. Granted, that is a significant range, but those ranges suggest that in most cases the gender dysphoria resolves.

However, most children whose dysphoria resolves report that they have a homosexual or bisexual orientation as they enter their teen years.[14] Among those children whose gender dysphoria desisted, a range from 63 percent to 100 percent of biological males and 32 percent to 50 percent of biological females identify as gay, lesbian or bisexual in adulthood. For example, in the Steensma et al. study,[15] all of the biological females whose gender dysphoria desisted reported a heterosexual orientation: "All girls felt exclusively attracted to boys. This made them question their 'masculine' feelings. It felt like the attractions weakened their cross-gender identification."[16] There was more variation among the biological males whose gender dysphoria desisted: "Two of the boys felt exclusively attracted to boys, three felt attracted to both boys and girls, and one boy reported feeling exclusively attracted to girls. The awareness of being sexually attracted to boys only or to both boys and girls caused some confusion in most of them."[17]

I have not spoken much about sexual orientation, but the apparent connection between the resolution of gender dysphoria and a homosexual or bisexual orientation is an interesting association in this line of research. As I mentioned earlier, the association between gender dysphoria and a bisexual or homosexual orientation has contributed to some of the concern about psychosocial intervention to prevent gender incongruence from continuing into adolescence or adulthood. As I mentioned above, the debates center on whether the resolution occurs "naturally," if you will.

Watchful waiting. One approach with children who exhibit signs of Gender Dysphoria is referred to as "watchful waiting" or a "wait and see" approach in which cross-gender behavior is permitted.[18] In that way, it contrasts with psychosocial interventions to reduce cross-gender behavior and identification, as it tries to be neutral in response to such expressions.

The primary difference between watchful waiting and facilitating a transition (which I will discuss below) is that there is not an a priori assumption in place that functions as a goal for the child's gender identity. Just as the watchful waiting approach is not attempting to reduce cross-gender behavior and identification, it is not intended as a means to reinforce cross-gender behavior and identification. Also, in addition to providing as neutral an environment as possible with respect to cross-gender behavior and identity, watchful waiting as an approach emphasizes helping the family attend to their anxiety about the outcome and to facilitate a positive view of self for the child.

One woman I know who experiences gender dysphoria and did so at a young age sees watchful waiting as "allowing God to do a spiritual, grace-filled work in the life of the child." From this perspective, allowing a child to explore various gender activities without imposing rigid gender stereotypes allows a child to gravitate toward his or her own interests. The boy who loves to cook is not gender dysphoric, but gender identity questions could arise in a context in which his father and peers ridicule him for his interest and relate to him out of rigid stereotypes that do not make room for his interests. I am not suggesting this causes gender dysphoria, but it can lead to unnecessary questioning of gender identity and potential damage that can come from placing arbitrary pressures on a child that are based more on parental fears than on anything else.

Psychosocial facilitation. The psychosocial facilitation approach facilitates social transition to the other gender.[19] While watchful waiting attempts to be neutral and does not hold out an end goal as an expectation for gender identity, psychosocial facilitation is considered "affirming" insofar as it practices out of several assumptions, including that "being transgender is not a mental illness."[20] Another assumption is that of outcome: either a "trans-adult outcome or a benign transition back to the original gender."[21]

As Drescher acknowledges, though little research has been conducted on this approach and these outcomes (what does a "benign transition back to the original gender" look like within one's peer group and community?), the approach reflects a supportive ("affirmative") posture that many mental health professionals would lean toward today.

According to Olson et al., "Affirmative approaches actively promote exploration of gender identity and assist adolescents and their families in learning about and engaging in appropriate gender transitioning interventions."[22] The social transitions here may or may not involve hormonal treatment, but they facilitate the exploration of the other gender with the intention of transition at some point. The elements involved in psychosocial facilitation could include "adoption of preferred gender hairstyles, clothing, and play, perhaps adopting a new name."[23]

When we talk about early social transition, the challenges that arise may be largely related to region of the country and relative support from one's family, peer group and other institutions, such as schools and religious institutions.

Puberty suppression. A more recent direction with older children and adolescents is the practice of puberty suppression or the use of hormone blockers (gonadotropin-releasing hormone analogs) to delay puberty. This is often connected to psychosocial facilitation of a cross-gender identity, as it would be the "next step" after early affirmation and social transition that would have stopped shy of hormone blocking.

How does it work? Children between the ages of ten and thirteen are prevented from entering puberty by receiving injections of hormone blockers that keep the gonads from making estrogen or testosterone. This, in turn, prevents the expected changes at puberty, such as girls developing breasts, starting their menstrual cycle, and so on. Boys will not grow body and facial hair, nor will their voice deepen. The idea is to then allow time for the child to enter into adolescence and for the teen (at around age sixteen) to eventually decide whether to develop a gender identity in accord with their birth sex or with their preferred/psychological/phenomenal sex.[24]

The original NPR report included an interview with Norman Spack, an endocrinologist at Children's Hospital in Boston:

> To put off puberty, children—usually between 10 and 13—are injected with hormone blockers once a month. Spack explains that the blockers only affect the gonads, the organs responsible for turning boys into men and girls into women. "If you can block the gonads, that is the ovary [in women] or the testis [in men], from making its sex steroids, that being estrogen or testosterone, then you can literally prevent . . . almost all the physical differences between the genders," Spack explains.
>
> Without testosterone, boys will not grow facial or body hair. Their voices will not deepen. There will be no Adams apple, and height growth will slow. Without estrogen, girls will not develop breasts, fat at the hip, or menstrual periods. And since most growth happens before puberty, if you block estrogen—and therefore puberty—girls will grow taller, closer to a typical male height.

The hormone blockers are the first stage of the treatment, but there's a second stage that's possible. Once children have postponed puberty for three or four years, at around age 16 they can choose to begin maturing sexually into the opposite gender, the gender they want to become. To do this, they begin taking the hormones of the opposite sex. For males, taking estrogen at this point will bring on breast and hip growth—and all the attributes physical and emotional of females. The reverse will happen for girls who take testosterone. Spack says this treatment can help make an adult transgender male almost indistinguishable from a biological male in terms of physical appearance.

Granted, there has been more recent discussion of moving that time up—that perhaps waiting until 16 is unnecessary, but that was the original idea. In any case, if they pursue their phenomenal sex, their preferred gender, they can begin to take the hormone of the opposite sex.

Proponents note that while this does not change a person's sex, it does provide what they claim is a smoother transition to the other gender insofar as the physical changes and appearance reflects such a transition. That transition, however, does not necessarily equate to improved mental health functioning or resolve comorbid mental health issues.

As I mentioned above, there has been research in support of both psychosocial intervention and puberty suppression. The NPR story cited above noted that researchers in the Netherlands have also been following children who underwent hormone-blocking treatment.[25] In their treatment of one hundred patients, all made the decision as adults to live as their phenomenal/felt/psychological gender (rather than their birth sex).[26]

Criticisms of puberty suppression range from concerns about the effects on bone-mass development to brain development to the concern mentioned previously about comorbid mental health issues not being resolved.[27] Sterility is also a concern.[28] Critics also express the preference that adolescents complete psychosexual development. Proponents of puberty suppression have pointed to the lack of consensus on what that is and how such advice is a response to the clinical dilemma of gender incongruence.[29] They have also admitted that more research is needed on possible effects on brain development, but that each of these concerns must also be weighed against risks associated with delaying intervention. Of course, if a transition were to occur later in life anyway, it is unclear whether delay in treatment would lessen those risks. At the same time, if there is still a possibility that gender dysphoria might abate at age twelve or thirteen, does the decision to use hormone blockers somehow preclude the possibility of natural desisting that might take place?

IN ADOLESCENCE

Aden came into our first session and made brief eye contact and then stared at the floor most of the time. Aden is a sixteen-year-old biological male whose parents brought him in for a consultation because for the past sixteen months he has insisted that he is female. In our first one-on-one meeting later that day, Aden shared that he would like to transition but that no one believes him. When I ask about "no one," he shares that he has confided in his parents, who are dismissive (saying things like, "But you're not a girl; you're a boy. It's that simple. You've always been a boy and you'll always be a boy!"). No one else knows. Aden shares that kids at school sometimes tease him for his outfits (which are essentially variations on the theme of black and foreboding) but do not seem to know about his cross-gender identification. Over the course of the next hour or so, we discussed when he first experienced the kind of incongruence he is now reporting, as well as the ebb and flow of various symptoms and how he has understood them in his life up to this point. We also discussed what he would like to see happen now, as well as what he anticipates and what he hopes to see happen in the next chapter of his life. I offered to answer questions he might have about research in this area, especially as he thinks about etiology and care at this point.

When considering treatment for adolescents, it should be noted that there is much less published research available to inform clinical decision making. This is part of what made the conversation with Aden difficult. As a general principle, from the time of assessment on, it is common to provide a place for honest self-disclosure of gender dysphoria and to address any shame associated with the experience of gender incongruence and associated secrecy. It would be common to assess the adolescent's emotional functioning, social support and related peer-group experiences, school performance, and family dynamics and functioning.[30]

It is not uncommon for older teens to be fairly familiar with the standards of care associated with gender identity concerns. By the time they come in for a consultation, they may have spent quite a bit of time researching the topic and identifying online communities for education and support. That was true with Aden. Clients may express interest in exploring a range of options now and in the future, including alternatives to the more invasive procedures, such as hormonal replacement therapy and sex-reassignment surgery. Therapy can explore the gender incongruence and dysphoria itself, questions regarding sexual orientation, and any comorbid mental health concerns, such as anxiety or depression, peer group disapproval, bullying, and so on.[31]

Exploration of the gender dysphoria includes an ongoing reflection of the meaning of the client's desire for sex-reassignment surgery and whether there are other, viable "lifestyle adaptations" available.[32] It is also important to explore whether the dysphoria is a negative response to homosexuality/same-sex sexuality rather than an actual desire to change one's sex. This is thought to be more often the case among those who express a strong desire for sex change closer to puberty.[33] In this case, it can be explored whether a homosexual adaption is possible, although this may not seem like a viable option for some for whom entering into same-sex relationships is also a concern.

As I mentioned above, puberty suppression is a more recent development in the management of gender dysphoria in older childhood and adolescence. I discussed it above as occurring "in childhood" because intervention begins when a child is between the ages of ten and thirteen. To extend that discussion of puberty suppression a little further, Olson and colleagues[34] discuss management of gender dysphoria in adolescence in three categories: *reversible, partially reversible* and *irreversible.* As I mentioned above, the *reversible* steps include adopting cross-gender hairstyles, clothing and interests, as well as perhaps use of a preferred name. This would have occurred in older childhood and would continue into adolescence, which is when puberty suppression would occur with gonadotropin-releasing hormone (GnRH) analogues.

The *partially reversible* step would be cross-gender hormone therapy (testosterone or estrogen depending on the direction of preferred gender identity).

The *irreversible* steps are surgical, of which there are a range, and I will discuss these under treatment of adults. Currently, most surgeons in the United States will not provide surgery until the adolescent turns eighteen.[35]

Aden presented with several co-occurring symptoms of distress, including anxiety and depression. Although it can be challenging to parse out what is co-occurring from what is subsequent to gender dysphoria, I felt it would be helpful for him to receive services that addressed several issues, including (1) teaching healthy coping and self-care strategies; (2) treating both anxiety and depression; (3) family therapy to improve the relationship that was at this time quite strained, and (4) helping him navigate gender identity questions in his life until he could be referred to a specialty clinic.

IN ADULTHOOD

Bert and Faye had been married some thirty years when they came to my office for a consultation. Each of their three children (two biological and one adopted) had been out of the house now for at least a couple of years, two were married, and one was now expecting their first grandchild. The reason they came for a consultation was Bert's relatively recent (within the past three years) revelation to Faye that he was a woman. This was really difficult for Faye to process. She would look at me and say, "Does this make any sense to you at all?" In a private meeting, Bert shared with me that he had known about his gender dysphoria for many years before he disclosed to Faye, but he had not known what it was before then. He thought he was losing his mind. He did not have a name for what he experienced, and that lack of understanding only inten-sified his confusion and distress. He has begun cross-dressing intermittently by wearing female undergarments. He is interested in presenting as female, but he and Faye agree that doing so locally would not be advisable. He has considered doing so on business trips, which he takes about every three to four weeks to larger cities around the country. He believes that this level of cross-gender identification will likely help him manage his dysphoria by helping him express who he experiences himself to be.

As the story of Bert and Faye exemplifies, the challenges in adult experiences of gender dysphoria are numerous and complex. When we look at outcomes for adult experiences of Gender Dysphoria, Carroll notes four typical outcomes: (1) unresolved outcomes, (2) biological sex and gender role, (3) engage in cross-gender behavior intermittently, or (4) adopt cross-gender role through sex reassignment.[36]

Unresolved outcomes simply reflect that there is a high attrition rate—estimated at up to half of clients who seek services—and this may be due to either personal ambivalence or frustration with what some have felt was a long and involved process (reflected in the current Standards of Care).[37] Others might drop out because of the cost of services. Still others may experience second thoughts about the best way to resolve their gender dysphoria. In his discussion of such ambivalence, Carroll writes:

Even though they may have made the initial effort to seek help, they may experience considerable doubt about their identity and, rather than explore these

issues in therapy, they may seek to reduce their distress by avoiding the exploration of their internal gender conflicts.[38]

It is unclear what happens to people who experience this level of doubt or ambivalence. Perhaps they find a way to manage their dysphoria, or perhaps they
find a way to compartmentalize gender identity concerns to function in life.

Others come to accept their biological sex and gender role (path 2). They
may feel gender dysphoric, but they live as their birth sex and adopt a lifestyle
that reflects that.[39] In the case of Bert and Faye, Bert shared that he would have
liked to have experienced some kind of resolution like this, especially if it
meant he and Faye could stay married and avoid predictable social stigma in
their rather small and conservative hometown. Faye definitely wanted this
resolution. Efforts here are placed on reducing a person's experience of gender
dysphoria. There are published care studies of such psychological resolutions.
However, as Carroll observes, "These claims have not been supported by controlled group studies. It appears now that the majority of adults with gender
dysphoria cannot, or will not, completely accept their given gender through
psychological treatment."[40]

Table 5.2. Gender Dysphoria: Pathways in Adulthood

Path 1: Undetermined outcome (an estimated 50% drop out of treatment due to frustration)		

⇩

Path 2	Path 3	Path 4
Resolve in accordance with their birth sex	Engage in cross-dressing behavior and role intermit-tently (often privately or in distant venues/locales)	Adopt cross-gender role and identity, which may include hormonal treatment and sex reassignment surgery

Carroll notes that psychological resolution appears to be more likely
among "a subgroup of cross-dressers with gender dysphoria." They may reflect
more of a fetish quality around cross-dressing, tend to be highly motivated
(whether such motivation is tied to work or marriage or family obligations),
and may conceptualize their concerns "from the perspective of a paraphilia or
sexual compulsion" whereby they respond to it with relevant cognitive and
behavioral strategies.[41]

The third outcome (path 3) is the most frequent outcome, that is, to engage
in cross-gender behaviors intermittently.[42] Bert did try this for several years.
For a biological male, this might mean growing his hair out longer, wearing

makeup occasionally, and cross-dressing either on the weekends or wearing female undergarments during the day to manage the dysphoria. For these men, cross-dressing is frequently related to sexual arousal (having more of a fetish quality that for some distinguishes it from a classic gender incongruence in which the person feels "trapped in the body of the other sex"). According to Carroll, "the majority of these men are heterosexual, often married, usually vocationally stable or successful."[43] The extent of cross-dressing behavior typically reflects the degree of dysphoria and how successfully such cross-dressing behaviors reduce the felt tension within.

The last outcome (path 4) is reflected in those who adopt the gender role of the opposite sex. They typically proceed to some full-time cross-gender identification. This may involve hormonal treatment and sex-reassignment surgery.[44] Throughout this whole process and again with the discussion of hormonal therapy and/or surgery, most mental health professionals reference the widely recognized Standards of Care of the World Professional Association for Transgender Health (WPATH; formerly referred to in the literature as the Harry Benjamin International Gender Dysphoria Standards of Care).[45]

The Standards note that the primary goal of therapy is "to find ways to maximize a person's overall psychological well-being, quality of life, and self-fulfillment."[46] Therapy "can help an individual to explore gender concerns and find ways to alleviate gender dysphoria, if present."[47] Emphasis may be on "clarifying and exploring gender identity and role,"[48] as well as responding to associated stressors and disclosure of gender identity–related matters to others in the person's life as appropriate.

To consider hormonal treatment or sex-reassignment treatment, a psychological evaluation is first conducted by a specialist in this area. The evaluation should assess mental/emotional health and gender identity.[49] It is strongly recommended (but not currently required) that a person then undergo a period of psychotherapy. The most recent recommendations do not offer a minimum number, as a number can be considered a "hurdle"; a number can detract from the ongoing work of providing services not just in the case of medical intervention; and a number does not speak to the relative differences in clients and clinicians in reaching the same goals in different time periods.[50]

If a person were to reach a point at which they were a candidate for surgery, it is recommended in the Standards of Care that they live for a year in the real-life experience of living full time as the desired gender.[51] Those twelve continuous months "allows for a range of different life experiences and events that may occur throughout the year (e.g., family events, holidays, vacations, season-specific work or school experiences)." The person would present in their preferred gender identity "consistently, on a day-to-day basis and across all settings of life. . . . This includes coming out to partners, family, friends, and community members (e.g., at school, work, other settings)."[52]

Table 5.3. Decision-Making Stages Regarding Sex Reassignment

Awareness	Characterized by distress related to Gender Dysphoria
Seeking information	Focus on education about Gender Dysphoria and identifying sources of support
Disclosure	Sharing with significant others one's diagnosis and experience of Gender Dysphoria
Exploration (identity and labeling)	Initial exploration of options for one's identity and identity label along a continuum
Exploration (transition issues)	Further exploration of identity, presentation and options regarding body modification (e.g., hormonal treatment, facial surgery, genital surgery)
Integration (post-transition issues)	Synthesis of identity in light of transition

(A. I. Lev, "Transgender Communities: Developing Identity Through Connection," in *Handbook of Counseling and Psychotherapy with Lesbian, Gay, Bisexual and Transgender Clients,* 2nd ed., ed. K. J. Bieschke, R. M. Perez and K. A. DeBord [Washington, DC: American Psychological Association, 2007], pp. 147-75.)

Lev[53] discusses a multi-stage model that reflects the kind of decision making a person faces when thinking about sex reassignment. It begins with awareness and moves through information seeking to disclosure to others and exploration of identity options and various issues that arise when giving serious consideration to transitioning. It ends with integration or the synthesis of an identity post-transition.

If we look back at the experience of Bert and Faye presented above, we see that Bert is in the place of exploration. He could identify a time of initial awareness of his gender dysphoria, and he shared how he had sought out information that helped him move beyond the initial thought he was losing his mind. He had also now disclosed to Faye and to an online community, as well as one local friend. Now he was exploring options for identity, which included some intermittent cross-gender attire. He was not at this time considering hair removal, hormonal treatment, or facial or genital surgery.

When I first read this multi-stage model of decision making, I was reminded of a study we had conducted of male-to-female transgender Christians[54] in which we asked about various milestones in their experiences of gender dysphoria. Not all were transsexuals, but some were and had gone through a similar decision-making model. Others were transgender and had not pursued hormonal treatment or sex-reassignment surgery.

As in the model proposed by Lev, there is a time of initial awareness about gender incongruence or dysphoria. In our sample, that was at about age six on average. That stage was followed by a time of internal confusion in which some shared that they engaged in cross-gender behavior; some received consequences for their behaviors or dress; and some reported an emotional dissonance that we believe was likely comparable to the gender dysphoria.

Table 5.4. Milestone Events for Male-to-Female Transgender Christians

Milestone	Age	Example
Awareness	6	Cross-dressing behaviors (n = 16); atypical play (n = 7)
Internal Confusion	11	External consequences (n = 6); gender variant behaviors (n = 6); emotional dissonance (n = 5)
Thoughts/Reasoning	18	Something is wrong with me (n = 8); need to do research (n = 6); wanted to be female (n = 5)
Attempts to Address Conflict	27	Sought counseling (n = 9); cross-dressing behaviors (n = 9)
Disclosure	35	Told spouse/significant other (n = 16)
Resolution	47	No resolution (n = 11); assistance from others (n = 9); transitioning (n = 9); acceptance (n = 6)

We also asked about how they made meaning out of their gender incongruence, and the more common answers had to do with something being wrong with them, needing to do research and wanting to be female. The "needing to do research" is similar to what Lev described as "seeking information." Participants in our study also shared about their attempts to address their gender identity conflict. The two most frequently cited attempts were by entering into counseling or engaging in cross-dressing behaviors.

Disclosure took place at an average age of thirty-five. It was typically to one's spouse. This is a stage that is also captured in Lev's decision-making model. The age of disclosure is likely to change dramatically in a cultural context in which younger people who experience gender dysphoria are more likely than the previous generation to know what their experiences mean in terms of contemporary conceptualizations and possible diagnoses.

In Lev's conceptualization, as a model of decision making regarding sex-reassignment surgery, the focus is on making that specific decision. In our study, we asked about resolution and found that many had not experienced a resolution. Some did transition, while others had not and were seeking assistance and support from others. In any case, it was an interesting study that lines up in some ways with what Lev describes in terms of stages. There are certainly key commonalities that a person could be aware of and provide support around, particularly how a person responds to their gender incongruence (both by attempts to address the conflict and by meaning-making structures) and issues surrounding disclosure and resolution, of which there are a range of possibilities.

In the care of adults, the WPATH standards outline several areas of responsibility for clinicians. The first is to follow the standards themselves. Other responsibilities are to make an accurate diagnosis of gender dysphoria and any comorbid conditions (and provide treatment for the comorbid concerns). Clinicians are to provide accurate information about a range of options and the implications of each. Therapy around these concerns is also to be provided. It is in the context of the therapeutic relationship that the clinician determines the client's readiness for hormone treatment and surgery, and this would at some point entail a more formal letter of recommendation (with relevant history documented) to colleagues in the medical and surgical fields. The clinician then serves as an important member of a multidisciplinary team, demonstrating collegiality to further the clinical care of the client. Care may be enhanced through education of family members, employers, faith communities and perhaps others. The clinician is then to be available for follow-up with the client as needed.

If the client has an intersex condition, many of the assessment and treatment issues are similar, overlapping with what we have already been discussing. However, these are different experiences. Tom Mazur and his colleagues note that the differences between those who have an intersex condition are significant and recommend that clinicians

> obtain a thorough history including chromosomal pattern, diagnosis, etiology (if known), surgeries, hormone treatment, pubertal development, and history of medications taken (up to and including current prescriptions). When obtaining a medical history, particular attention should be paid to factors believed to be associated with gender change in persons with intersex. Questions to ask might include the following: Did the person have late (after age of three years)

or no genital surgery? If the person is an adolescent or adult, is their puberty (secondary sexual characteristics) discordant with their assigned gender? Is the person sexually attracted to individuals of the same gender, meaning the gender to which the person with intersex was initially assigned?[55]

Indeed, the *DSM-5* would have clinicians note an intersex condition noted under the diagnosis of Gender Dysphoria. The clinician is still assessing readiness for possible sex-reassignment surgery. However, there are important differences that may have more to do with psychological issues if the person was assigned a sex at birth, raised in that gender role and then comes to a different phenomenological experience of themselves later in life.

Some people with an intersex condition may pursue sex-reassignment surgery with the intention of identifying as the other gender; others will identify as intersex. Still others may choose to live as the gender they believe they are psychologically without pursuing surgery for a number of reasons.[56]

Most people who are unfamiliar with Gender Dysphoria may make assumptions about surgical options. There are actually a number of surgical procedures available, although the most frequently discussed for the biological male who is transitioning is vaginoplasty or the creation of a neovagina (with a penectomy or the removal of the penis and orchiectomy or the removal of the testes). Male hair can also be removed, and corrective surgery can be performed on the larynx. Surgery to enhance the breasts (breast augmentation) can also be performed. People vary considerably on which surgeries (if any) they have done. For the biological female, the breasts, uterus and ovaries can be removed. Some patients will also request phalloplasty or the creation of a neophallus. If the patient has an enlarged clitoris (sometimes as a result of taking male hormones), it may be cut loose in a way that it can be experienced more like a penis (metaidioplasty).

Many adults who are diagnosed with Gender Dysphoria do not undergo any of these surgeries. They may not be prepared to do something as permanent and complete, or they may believe that their dysphoria is manageable without taking such steps. Some people who undergo some of the surgical procedures do not undergo all of the options that are available to them. When interacting with people who are navigating these decisions, unless there is a clinical rationale for asking about specific surgical procedures, I recommend letting the person tell their story in their time, including sharing from their experience about the decisions they have made, rather than initiating with a line of questions or out of any attempt to satisfy one's curiosity. In my experience listening to transsexual persons, being asked about these surgical procedures can be experienced as a rather invasive line of questioning that no one else is subjected to.

One author reports that about three-fourths or more of those who complete sex-reassignment surgery report satisfaction with their new identity and only about 8 percent report poor outcomes with surgery.[57] Others have reported that only about 2 percent actually regret sex-reassignment surgery with 4 percent expressing dissatisfaction with the surgical outcomes.[58] A recent study that examined outcomes over a fifty-year period in Sweden (1960–2010) indicated a 2.2 percent rate of regret for both MtF and FtM transsexual persons.[59]

One way to look at figures that indicate a fairly high degree of satisfaction is that they reflect a funnel that begins broad with those who first seek help due to their gender dysphoria, particularly as the dysphoria rises to a level of significant distress or impairment. Once properly diagnosed with Gender Dysphoria, they face several options as they now have a name and way of conceptualizing what they experience. This is followed by those who then might consider the removal of body hair and some cross-sex identification on a part-time basis. Then, over the course of time, as various considerations arise—experiences in therapy, experiences with one's family and peer group, experiences in part-time cross-gender role and especially full-time cross-gender role (or "lived informed consent"[60]), issues associated with cost, and so on—some people will be more likely to consider voice/vocal training (if they have not done so yet) and one or more surgical procedures.

What we know at this point is that those with a female-to-male conversion report adjusting better, on average, than those whose conversion is male-to-female, although again there is great variability. Many people attribute this to it being easier to "pass" when a person has transitioned from female-to-male rather than male-to-female. Older persons pursuing reassignment do not report having as favorable outcomes as younger persons.[61]

Also, those who follow the Blanchard typology report that more autogynephilic transsexual presentations end up regretting their sex reassignment than those who have been understood to be androphilic transsexuals, and this may reflect the tendency to be "less strongly driven by gender dysphoria than full-blown transsexuals."[62] In other words, if a person's experience of gender incongruence is not of a classic transsexual presentation but has a more paraphilic quality about it, the best resolution may very well not be sex-reassignment surgery but rather other psychosocial interventions that address the association with arousal. Lawrence[63] discusses options that fall short of sex-reassignment surgery, although there are complexities with autogynephilic expressions (e.g., not all wish to live full time as the other sex) that may make it difficult to complete the Standards of Care as they are currently written.

As one might imagine, better outcomes and rates of satisfaction among those who go through sex-reassignment surgery are related to positive surgical outcomes, as well as consistent use of hormones.[64] One female-to-male transgender person I spoke to shared that he had the chest reconstruction surgery to address the primary source of gender dysphoria but had not had additional ("lower" or "bottom") surgery and was working in therapy on the treatment of body dysmorphia (preoccupation or significant concerns) associated with his current state.

Although previous research[65] on follow-up of transsexual persons tended to be rather favorable, researchers tended not to follow the person over a long period of time. A more recent study[66] that provided data on long-term follow-up reported increased risks for suicide attempts, death from suicide, and psychiatric inpatient care that are "considerably higher risks" than the general population.

> This study found substantially higher rates of overall mortality, death from cardio-vascular disease and suicide, suicide attempts, and psychiatric hospitalizations in sex-reassigned transsexual individuals compared to a healthy control population. This highlights that post surgical transsexuals are a risk group that need long-term psychiatric and somatic follow-up. Even though surgery and hormonal therapy alleviates gender dysphoria, it is apparently not sufficient to remedy the high rates of morbidity and mortality found among transsexual persons.[67]

These are sobering findings that raise the question of whether these more invasive procedures are the answer for transsexuality. Perhaps other options should be explored further. Perhaps indicative of the broader support for this direction of care in the mental health field, the authors of the study took the position that greater emphasis should be placed on aftercare and longer-term support following surgery: "Improved care for the transsexual group after the sex reassignment should therefore be considered."[68]

CONCERNS ABOUT SEX-REASSIGNMENT SURGERY

I distinctly remember the time I finished a talk I had given on sexual identity. I had been asked a question about gender identity (which is not uncommon after an extended discussion of sexual identity), and apparently my response raised more questions than answers. Two men in the audience came up to talk to me. The one introduced himself and his friend and shared with me that his friend had transitioned from male to female years ago, later became a Christian and eventually felt he needed to reclaim his identity as a male. The former male-to-female transsexual did not say much and seemed rather socially reserved, but we talked a little about the concerns he had as a new Christian that led him to conclude he needed to transition back.

I bring up this example to point out that not everyone is supportive of cross-gender identification with or without surgery. In the case of surgical procedures, though, people have articulated concerns about sex-reassignment surgery. Some concerns have to do with long-term outcomes and comorbidity, as noted above. Even here, however, many researchers are not so much questioning the surgery but the level of support provided after surgery is completed, suggesting an overall trend in professional support for hormonal treatment and sex-reassignment surgery.

However, the philosophical position that supports sex-reassignment surgery for gender dysphoria is not without its critics. For example, McHugh wrote a strong criticism of the practice of sex-reassignment surgery, pointing out that the fact that we can do such surgeries does not mean we ought to do such surgeries:

> The skills of our plastic surgeons, particularly on the genito-urinary system, are impressive. They were obtained, however, not to treat the gender identity problem, but to repair congenital defects, injuries, and the effects of destructive diseases such as cancer in this region of the body.[69]

Indeed, McHugh goes on to suggest that psychiatry has essentially catered to individual preferences and cultural pressure—"fashions of the seventies that invaded the clinic";[70] he likens sex-reassignment surgery to liposuction for anorexics:

> It is not obvious how this patient's feeling that he is a woman trapped in a man's body differs from the feeling of a patient with anorexia nervosa that she is obese despite her emaciated, cachetic state. We don't do liposuction on anorexics.

Why amputate the genitals of these poor men? Surely, the fault is in the mind not the member.[71]

McHugh elaborated on his argument in a more recent opinion piece in *The Wall Street Journal*:

> The transgendered suffer a disorder of "assumption" like those in other disorders familiar to psychiatrists. With the transgendered, the disordered assumption is that the individual differs from what seems given in nature—namely one's maleness or femaleness. Other kinds of disordered assumptions are held by those who suffer from anorexia and bulimia nervosa, where the assumption that departs from physical reality is the belief by the dangerously thin that they are overweight.[72]

A similar argument was brought up in the popular press. In an article that first appeared in the *Chicago Sun-Times* and was later retracted, Kevin D. Williamson wrote about sex-reassignment surgery. He was discussing Katie Couric's interview of Laverne Cox, a transgender person who had been featured on the cover of *Time* magazine:

> Regardless of the question of whether he has had his genitals amputated, Cox is not a woman, but an effigy of a woman. Sex is a biological reality, and it is not subordinate to subjective impressions, no matter how intense those impressions are, how sincerely they are held, or how painful they make facing the biological facts of life. No hormone injection or surgical mutilation is sufficient to change that.
>
> Genital amputation and mutilation is the extreme expression of the phenomenon, but it is hardly outside the mainstream of contemporary medical practice. The trans self-conception, if the autobiographical literature is any guide, is partly a feeling that one should be living one's life as a member of the opposite sex and partly a delusion that one is in fact a member of the opposite sex at some level of reality that transcends the biological facts in question. There are many possible therapeutic responses to that condition, but the offer to amputate healthy organs in the service of a delusional tendency is the moral equivalent of meeting a man who believes he is Jesus and inquiring as to whether his insurance plan covers crucifixion.[73]

In the final analysis, the argument from critics of sex-reassignment surgery as treatment for gender identity concerns is that more effort should be placed on prevention and management of gender dysphoria: "We have to learn how to manage this condition as a mental disorder when we fail to prevent it."[74]

Another consideration has to do with whether we are providing the best care to those who have more of an autogynephilic presentation. They appear to be at greater risk for regretting the decision to pursue sex reassignment. Should there be a more complete assessment and nuanced decision tree around pursuing the most invasive treatment given the greater risk that it may not be gender dysphoria that is actually driving the request for surgery? The argument has been made by Lawrence[75] in the other direction, that is, that perhaps a more nuanced assessment would allow for sex-reassignment surgery for those autogynephilic men who are actually unable to complete the full-time presentation as a female, thus giving greater weight to autogynephilic motivations.

As I mentioned, while there are critics of sex-reassignment surgery, the trend within the mental health field is toward such an intervention when indicated. However, most people who experience gender incongruence in adulthood do not undergo surgery. Most cross-dress intermittently either as an expression of their sense of gender identity or they use cross-dressing as a way to manage their dysphoria, among other possible motivations.

CONCLUDING THOUGHTS

As I think about prevention and intervention in childhood, adolescence and adulthood, I want to return to the integrated framework for understanding gender incongruence. Recall that the framework draws from the following three frameworks or lenses through which we might view gender dysphoria:

- The *integrity* framework, which identifies the phenomenon of gender incongruence as confusing the sacredness of maleness and femaleness and specific resolutions as violations of that integrity.

- The *disability* framework, which identifies gender incongruence as a reflection of a fallen world in which the condition is a disability, a nonmoral reality to be addressed with compassion.

- The *diversity* framework, which highlights transgender issues as reflecting an identity and culture to be celebrated as an expression of diversity.

The integrity framework reminds us why it may be important to at least consider managing a child's environment in a way that does not reinforce cross-gender behavior and identity. Having worked with parents around the presentation of a child's cross-gender identity and behavior, redirecting a child's behaviors and ways of relating is a challenge for parents who may otherwise wish to affirm an integrity framework, as it can be experienced as going against what seems to come almost naturally to the child. This can create ambivalence for parents who also love and want to find practical ways to support their child. These parents might be drawn to more of a watchful waiting approach to what appears to be gender incongruence.

The integrity framework would give the Christian pause when thinking of puberty suppression. That is not to say a Christian parent would not consider such an intervention, but the integrity framework reminds them to think through several issues before making that kind of decision, particularly if suppression was recommended to start at or prior to the time when an older child's experiences of gender dysphoria could yet desist. That decision could be a remarkably difficult and painful one, and consultation with experts in this area would be important.

The disability framework reminds us to demonstrate great compassion and empathy as we think about a child who is displaying signs of gender dysphoria. It also reminds us to be supportive of parents who may feel quite isolated and ashamed, as though they were concerned that people in their community would think that they caused the gender identity concerns.

Although perhaps not as critical for identity in childhood, the weak form of the diversity framework reminds us of meaning-making structures and how our understanding of gender dysphoria needs to also be affirmative of a young child's value and dignity. When we fail to provide a sense of meaning and purpose and pathways to identity and community in these other frameworks, we cannot act surprised or offended when people opt for the benefits they find in the diversity framework.

The integrated framework is also critical in adolescence and adulthood. Let me talk about the integrity framework and the disability framework together. The integrity framework gives us pause about the most invasive procedures here. But what does that mean? Many people I have known who experience gender dysphoria have found it helpful, in keeping with a disability framework, to think of ways they can learn to manage their gender dysphoria. Different behaviors or dress may not be ideal, but the person identifies the least invasive way to manage their dysphoria so that it does not become too distressing or impairing. This places such management on a continuum from least to most invasive and recognizes that hormonal treatment and sex reassignment would be the most invasive. This is not to say a Christian would not consider the most invasive procedures; I know many who have. But they would not begin there, nor would they take such a decision lightly. Ideally, they would consider options based upon the input and recommendations from experts in this area, as well as thoughtful and prayerful consideration with a discernment group of those whose perspectives they respect.

The diversity framework raises questions of personal value, worth and dignity. It is particularly important because the disability framework does not do all that much for a sense of identity. Most people do not find, "I'm managing my dysphoria in the least invasive way" as a particularly meaningful storyline for identity and community. Recall that the trends toward transitioning are affirming precisely because they help to answer questions about identity and community in ways that truly resonate with a person's psychological and emotional experience of their gender identity. Any attempt at intervention in adolescence and adulthood would benefit from reflecting a meaning-making structure that informs identity and locates the person within a broader community of support. This community would function as a kind of kinship network (family) that affirms their worth and insists on navigating this terrain together, even when decisions may be quite complex and challenging to all involved.

6

Toward a Christian Response

At the Level of the Individual

LET ME SHARE THE STORY of another person whom I know as Blake, a female-to-male transgender person who was formerly known to others as Brooklyn:

> Brooklyn struggled with gender dysphoria from a young age. She was born and raised in a small town in the South, where she was brought up in a fundamentalist church. Her parents took creative steps to present toys and games and attire to match her birth sex as female. They would offer a few toys, and Brooklyn "always" preferred the stereotypically boy games (e.g., action figures, Matchbox cars, toy guns), despite always having at least one option that was more stereotypically for girls (e.g., Barbie, baby dolls). Brooklyn shared how her preferences for cross-sex toys/games/attire kept bumping up against their expectations for gender identity and role. Over the next several years, as Brooklyn's interests persisted, Brooklyn's parents struggled with whether her cross-sex-typed interests meant she was going to hell. They saw nothing other than condemnation in her presentation and interests. "They could not see me," Brooklyn shared with me. As a result, this was a huge fear of hers for many years. Brooklyn struggled in not finding acceptance within her religion, and she struggled with a strong desire to take her life that persisted through college and beyond. During those years, Brooklyn managed her dysphoria initially by presenting as a lesbian and by wearing very masculine attire through college. These experiences were "okay" for a time but ultimately dissatisfying as they did not seem to address the more fundamental concerns.
>
> In one of her darkest moments, it was her grandfather, a fundamentalist Christian and patriarch of the family, who spoke new life into her when he said, "You'll have to find a path to God that will work for you, and it's going to be hard. It won't be the same path I took." Brooklyn shed tears that had been pent up for years. She had not

known that there was still a path to God for her. She would later begin the long
process of transitioning. Brooklyn shared with me that the word "transitioning" sug-
gests everyone does all of the same things to present in a cross-sex manner. Not so. As
Brooklyn reflected on the meaning of that word, she said, "Each person considers
what transitioning is for that person." For Brooklyn, it has meant some surgery
(chest) and some use of hormones but not much more at this time. Brooklyn even-
tually adopted the name Blake, a favorite name that was associated in his mind with
his grandfather. He eventually decided to explore that path to God his grandfather
had spoken of and found a church, Bible study and small group that would create
room for him to study and pray and share life together. He disclosed to his pastor and
was told, "You are welcome here." He is now beginning to explore a path to God and
find a way forward after years of searching.

Blake presents the church with a remarkable challenge. It is hard to know
what is best for someone who is navigating gender dysphoria from such a
young age and in a way that leads to self-destructive thoughts. A place to begin
to is to come to a better understanding of the phenomenon that the person
you are talking to experiences. I hope this book has provided information that
will help you toward that end. You will learn a lot, too, from listening to the
person's story.

When it comes to meeting with someone who is navigating gender identity
concerns, I rely on elements of narrative therapy. Narrative therapy focuses on
the role of socially constructed "scripts" in a person's life. What is perhaps most
interesting about narrative approaches to therapy is that they are often used with
marginalized groups whose "story" has been written by a dominant culture: "On
a larger level, entire groups of people could have their story about themselves
completely overtaken by a more dominant group story about them."[1]

In their description of narrative therapy, Zimmerman and Dickerson describe the ways in which cultural stories can create narratives that can lead to
difficulties for the person:

> Cultural stories determine the dimensions that organize people's experience.
> These narratives about what is canonical provide a backdrop against which ex-
> periences are interpreted. Cultural stories are not neutral. . . . They lead to con-
> structions of a normative view, generally reflecting the dominant culture's
> specifications, from which people know themselves and against which people
> compare themselves.[2]

Most mainstream, secular narrative approaches to gender dysphoria would posit that it is the sex and gender binary that is oppressive to the person who is gender dysphoric. This is an interesting perspective steeped largely in the strong form of the diversity framework, and it is something that needs to be argued for rather than assumed to be the case.

In any case, I do not use narrative therapy with that set of philosophical assumptions. However, because interpretation is so important in narrative approaches, I do see benefit in some of the techniques that can inform meaning making and decisions about identity and gender. For example, I find it helpful when I first meet with someone who experiences gender dysphoria to map gender identity conflicts in their life, both current conflicts and the person's history with those conflicts.

MAPPING GENDER IDENTITY CONFLICTS

Recall that we do not know what causes these various experiences of gender incongruence. Indeed, the range of presentations should give us pause that

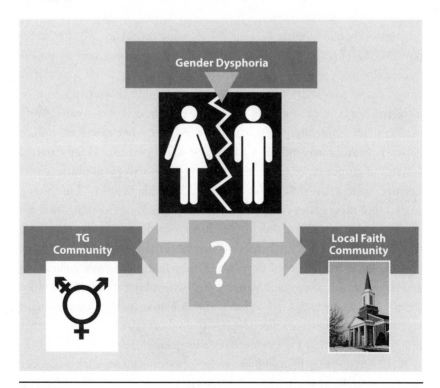

Figure 6.1.

any one theory of etiology will suffice. There are likely multiple influences that are weighted differently for different people, and these influences likely contribute to a range of outcomes.

The first consideration in mapping gender identity conflicts raises the question, *How does the person experience his or her gender identity concerns?* What is it like for this person in particular? Besides asking the person to share more about their experiences, one thing that can be helpful is gauging a person's experience of gender incongruence, as well as a person's sense for how they are managing that incongruence.

Although we are focusing here on the experience of gender dysphoria in terms of strength of incongruence and capacity to manage it, keep in mind that the gender identity concerns, while important, may not be the greatest concern in this person's life. Consider together whether there are other pressing issues to attend to, such as a marriage or relationships with family members or personal walk with God, education, and so on. Too often Christians can focus almost exclusively on the very aspect of the person with which we are most uncomfortable.

In a workbook I recently developed with some colleagues, we offer an opportunity to reflect on these two experiences in a way that recognizes the differences between sense of incongruence and one's ability to live with that incongruence.[3] We invite a person to identify their subjective sense of incongruence as well as their subjective sense of distress. A person can identify ways in which gender dysphoria has influenced him or her, as well as how the person has influenced gender identity concerns. The person can keep a journal and record various experiences over the next couple of weeks in which gender identity concerns are influencing them. A person might write, "I feel preoccupied with these issues every day. It's hard to focus on other things that are also important to me." Another person might record the following: "I get discouraged. Sometimes I feel shame, like I am not who I should be."

A person can also record times when they find themselves influencing gender dysphoria. They could write, "I feel better about my gender identity when I spend time with God. When I pray, it helps." Another person might say, "It has helped to serve other people—to do short-term missions and other things like that. I think I get a glimpse of a bigger picture."

An illustration may help with mapping. A person who experiences gender dysphoria can be invited to imagine his or her computer screen or cell phone screen and the small icons that are present on the screen. These icons are small when they are minimized at the bottom or side of the screen, but they are always there. They can be double-clicked and an icon's application, file or folder will occupy the entire screen. The size of the icon, or how it reacts on the screen, is up to the person. The person can then be invited to think of their experiences of gender dysphoria as an "icon on the computer screen."[4] What they can begin to track are the times and experiences in which the icon of their gender dysphoria is essentially "double-clicked"—the experiences that make their gender dysphoria larger, so that it occupies the entire screen. It may also be helpful to journal events, experiences, thoughts and so on that seem to keep the icon of gender dysphoria smaller on the screen. This essentially means that the person's experience of gender dysphoria is more manageable.

1) Make a mark on the first line below (which shows a continuum from low to very high) that shows your *current* sense of incongruence.

2) Then, make a mark on the second line below that shows your *current* sense of your own ability to live with, and handle, a sense of incongruence.

My sense of gender incongruence:

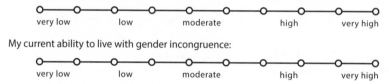

My current ability to live with gender incongruence:

Figure 6.2. Monitoring gender incongruence

Taken further, if there are other icons on the screen—that is, other icons that represent parts of the person—these can also be explored in a journal or in discussions with a counselor. If the person has some success minimizing the icon called "gender dysphoria" (that is, not focusing on it exclusively), could they then see other icons that represent parts of themselves, which might allow them to maximize the other icons of interest?

- Write about when you might maximize/blow up the "gender dysphoria icon."

- What is it like for you when your gender dysphoria is "double-clicked" and takes up the entire "screen" of your life?

- Write about when you might minimize/reduce the "gender dysphoria icon."

- What is it like for you when your gender dysphoria is "minimized" and you are able to see the other "icons" on the "screen" of your life?[5]

This kind of exercise may be helpful to some people who experience gender identity conflicts, particularly those for whom their dysphoria ebbs and flows. Those who may not find it as helpful are those for whom the experiences of gender dysphoria do not respond to any kind of discernible pattern, in which case the minimizing and maximizing can be more confusing and frustrating.

Another exercise some people find helpful is to interview their concern. This involves identifying and externalizing the conflict they experience in their gender identity and talking to it as though it were a person who could share its thoughts and experiences. A person could ask the following questions in an interview of his or her gender identity concerns: In what areas of my life have you been causing me difficulties? In what ways have you affected my relationship with God? In what areas do I seem to get the best of you?

It may also be helpful to ask the person to draw their gender identity concerns, particularly how they see these concerns during an interview. Are they having a quiet discussion in a coffee shop? Or is this more like an interrogation at police headquarters? Those two images alone would communicate volumes about how the person experiences his or her gender identity conflicts.

ATTRIBUTIONAL SEARCH REGARDING GENDER IDENTITY

In addition to mapping gender identity concerns, it can be helpful to reflect with a person on gender identity and meaning making. This is referred to as "attributional search" or joining a person on an attributional search regarding gender identity. The central question associated with attributional search is: *How does the person make sense of his or her gender incongruence?* This is more a question of meaning making. I often illustrate this as a person asking the question about what all of this means. For example, in chapter two I introduced three different explanatory frameworks: integrity, disability and diversity frameworks. In terms of meaning making, an integrity framework might be reflected in a person who experiences gender incongruence as a concern because he or she is a Christian who views the incongruence as a reflection of a fallen world.

A disability framework might share this perspective—that the disability is what one may find from time to time in a fallen world. It is essentially a nonmoral reality in a world that is touched in so many different ways by sin. It is not the person who has sinned—anymore than we would think of the person who has any other medical or psychiatric condition as having sinned in terms of being personally responsible for the phenomenon.

Finally, when we look at the diversity framework, we can make a distinction between the strong and weak forms of the framework. Recall that the strong form may be voiced by some transgender advocates who wish to deconstruct sex and gender. The weak form is primarily interested in how to address questions of identity and community among those who experience gender dysphoria. In my view, one of the overlooked benefits to the weak form of the diversity framework is that it provides an affirmation of identity and community, two important considerations for anyone who is navigating gender identity concerns.

COMPETING MESSAGES

The transgender community is rather unique. In some regards it is part of the gay community. The popular string of identity labels is lesbian, gay, bisexual and transgender (LGBT). However, persons who identify as transgender often report some point of tension with the gay community, too, as reactions to actual transgender persons vary widely.

Generally speaking, however, the transgender community sends a very affirming message to another person who is navigating gender identity issues. I refer to these messages as cultural scripts. A script is a cultural expectation for behavior and meaning making. In most settings, there is a cultural expectation to behave a certain way, for example, as with a congregation listening to a pastor deliver a sermon. There is a cultural expectation for an audience listening to a speaker at a TED Talk. These cultural expectations are scripts. From a narrative perspective, a script is essentially a storyline that can shape behavior but also provides messages imbued with meaning and purpose. I suggested in an earlier work that there is something like a gay script for people who experience same-sex attractions. A gay script contains expectations for both behavior and meaning making. Something akin to that can be identified in discussions about gender identity too.

Storylines from the transgender community. There is a kind of script from the transgender community (what I will refer to as a "TG script") that helps people make sense of themselves and locate themselves in a broader transgender community. How does that script read?

- Gender dysphoria reflects a naturally occurring difference among types of people (transgender rather than cisgender).

- Your gender dysphoria as gender incongruence suggests who you are (*"who* I am") rather than how you are (*"how* I am").

- Gender dysphoria points to a community of others who experience a similar phenomenon ("I am part of the transgender community").

- Your gender incongruence points to something at the core of who you are, something that is central to your identity.

The general message picked up as a TG script is that the gender incongruence is important data that tells the person something about identity. The dysphoria may signal who the person "is"—that is, "who I am." A person can take that in a number of directions, but the idea is that "I was born in the wrong body; the person I am is inside of me, and I need to express that." The person has a sense of identity (who I am; I am transgender) and a sense of community: "I am part of the transgender community," which could mean different things to different people.

If we were to visually illustrate this script, we would see that the diversity framework is given considerable weight relative to the integrity framework and the disability framework.

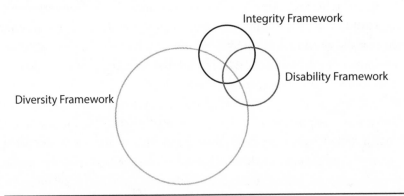

Figure 6.3. The TG script

A person often receives the message that they are born this way. As I discussed in chapter three, scientists do not know what causes gender incongruence. It is a rare phenomenon and one in which we have little by way of research to inform the discussion. A popular theory is the brain-sex theory, but there are gaps in our understanding of that theory too. There is likely no one causal path that accounts for the many and varied experiences that fall under the transgender umbrella as well as what we see as a continuum of gender incongruence, even among those for whom incongruence is the more salient experience.

Another part of the TG script is that the gender incongruence forms the core of that person's identity. It is central to that person's sense of self. Again, that could take the form of "being transgender" as the identity in and of itself, or it could signal who they are if they were to express themselves as the other sex. This view lends itself to expression of one's true self in behavior, attire and role.

If we try to illustrate the TG script in a Venn diagram, we see that the script relies primarily (and, in many cases, almost exclusively) on the diversity framework. It answers important questions about identity and community. The integrity framework is also in play for those who see an essential maleness and femaleness as part of the discussion but believe that the brain-sex theory explains how what is essential is in a cross-gender-identified brain that is in contrast with anatomy. The disability framework may also be a part of the discussion insofar as the person who experiences gender dysphoria finds the diagnosis of Gender Dysphoria helpful to them by providing them with the language and conceptualization to explain what has been inexplicable to them.

Storylines from the local Christian community. In contrast to the transgender script, the local Christian community also extends a script to those who experience gender incongruence. The backdrop to the messages frequently sent from the Christian community is fairly rigid stereotypes about what it means to be male or female. These inform gender roles that are difficult for some people to live in, particularly if a person does not have stereotypical presentation or interests.

That cultural backdrop informs a message with expectations for those who experience gender incongruence. The messages vary somewhat from person to person, but the general message has included things like:

- This is a spiritual matter; this is sinful.

- Fulfillment comes from adopting a traditional gender role that corresponds with your biological sex.

- The failure to find worth and purpose and meaning in traditional gender roles and expressions is a mark of willful disobedience.

- Cross-gender behaviors and roles are unacceptable as they undermine the truth about who you have been made to be.

There are two primary messages from the local church regarding gender dysphoria. One has to do with gender dysphoria as sin, and in many cases this has been conveyed as though the gender dysphoria itself were a sign of willful disobedience. The second message from the evangelical Christian community is often to find worth and purpose and meaning in traditional gender roles, and that failure to do so is sin. As a person seeks ways to navigate their gender incongruence and perhaps manage their dysphoria in the least invasive ways possible, they see few options as acceptable to fellow Christians, as those "least invasive" approaches may be viewed as going against the created order and deemed sinful.

Ultimately, these messages communicate shame to the person navigating gender identity concerns. Shame is the psychological and emotional experience of believing yourself to be inadequate in ways that lead you to reject yourself. It hides itself from others on the assumption that if others knew this about the person, they too would reject them.

If we illustrate the conservative religious script in a Venn diagram, we see that the integrity framework is the prominent lens through which gender dysphoria is seen. The disability framework may be a consideration insofar as conservative religious people can conceptualize gender dysphoria as a mental health concern that may reflect a unique way in which the fall has touched the person, but this script does not draw on the diversity framework, and may even be suspicious that the disability framework ultimately relies on assumptions from the diversity framework.

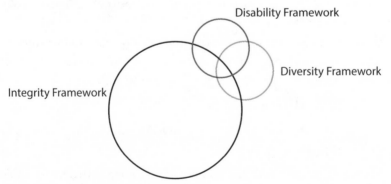

Figure 6.4. The conservative religious script

A study conducted of transgender Christians asked about pain they experienced from their faith community as they navigated gender identity issues in their lives. One participant wrote: "The negative messages from the Church did irreparable harm to my self-esteem that took most of my life to recover from."[6] Speaking to the isolation that often accompanies shame, another participant simply wrote: "It kept me hidden for years."[7]

Other possible storylines. As Christians consider a response to the person who is navigating gender identity concerns, it may be helpful to introduce other possible storylines. I am thinking here of storylines that contrast with the TG script and the script from the local conservative community of faith.

- Experiences of gender dysphoria are part of my reality (that is, "how I am").

- I did not choose to experience gender dysphoria or gender incongruence, and I honestly do not know the cause.

- Perhaps being transgender is part of my identity; however, I am a complex person and am more than gender dysphoric.

- I do not know how I came to experience gender dysphoria, but I can consider what it means to me today and where I go from here.

- There are probably a dozen different directions for any experience of gender dysphoria, and I plan to consider many of them, and may select some of them, considering the least invasive steps when possible.

Again, this list of possible other storylines is not exhaustive. What it does is "thicken the plot" of the existing TG narrative as well as the storyline from the local community of faith.

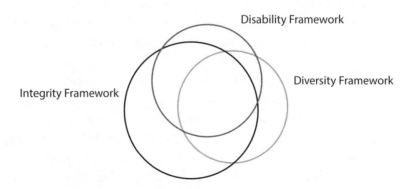

Figure 6.5. Other possible storylines

How do these other possible storylines look with reference to the integrative framework that seeks the best from the integrity, disability and diversity frameworks? It's unclear whether there is one way to best illustrate this. I imagine this could vary from setting to setting and individual to individual as it is tailored to what motivates each person's cross-gender identification as well as what it means to manage the dysphoria. These are the lenses through which we look, and we can be thoughtful about these ratios—what we need to consider—and how these considerations will be applied.

The Venn diagram changes when we consider other possible storylines. I am not suggesting that the integrity framework is exactly equal in weight and application to the diversity framework or the disability framework, but they will overlap much more here. Perhaps different people with different presentations will draw from us different ratios of consideration in ministry. The disability framework can help the church foster greater compassion and empathy for the person navigating gender dysphoria. The integrity framework is still an important consideration for the Christian, and it may even inform meaning-making structures that have not been fully identified but may be related to the diversity framework and are absent in the disability framework.

A MULTI-TIER DISTINCTION

One exercise that some people find helpful is to discuss a multi-tier distinction in language and meaning. In the multi-tier model, one way to describe a person's experience is to simply say, "I am a person who experiences gender incongruence." This is perhaps the most descriptive way to communicate part of a person's experience.

A second way to describe one's experience is to say, "I am someone who is transgender" or "I am a transgender person." This is the use of *transgender* as an adjective. It describes *how* a person is (in contrast to identity as such).

A third approach to language and meaning is to say, "I am transgender." This use of language communicates identity; it is the use of the word *transgender* as identity, that is, *who* a person is.

The last approach to language and meaning in this multi-tier approach is to say, "I am transgender, which I define as. . . ." This is the use of *transgender* with an added personal definition to communicate more accurately who you are and how you understand that identity and what weight or significance it is given at the same time.

Table 6.1. A Multi-Tier Distinction in Language and Meaning

	Language	Meaning
Tier 1	"I am a person who experiences gender dysphoria."	The most descriptive way to convey part of your experience.
Tier 2	"I am someone who is transgender" or "I am a transgender person."	Use of *transgender* as an adjective; describing how you are.
Tier 3	"I am transgender."	Use of *transgender* as identity. This is who you are.
Tier 4	"I am transgender, which I define as . . ."	Use of *transgender* and a personal definition to more accurately define who and how you are at the same time.

It is also possible that identity labels are used based on situation. Some transgender persons will identify as such in front of a class to teach them what the term means, how they experience their gender identity and how other expressions might fit under the transgender umbrella. However, that same person might not identify as transgender in any other setting.

While gender identity is more fluid than biological sex, when we have cases in which a person experiences gender dysphoria, what is the best way to proceed? Although the body of Christ should resist rigid stereotypes of gender that might be unbearably restrictive, I also want to reiterate a cultural shift that may contribute to greater uncertainty around sex and gender.[8] Toward that end, I see the value in encouraging individuals who experience gender dysphoria to resolve dysphoria in keeping with their birth sex. Where those strategies have been unsuccessful, there is potential value in managing dysphoria through the least invasive expressions (recognizing surgery as the most invasive step toward expression of one's internal sense of identity). Given the complexities associated with these issues and the potential for many and varied presentations, pastoral sensitivity should be a priority.

TELLING OTHERS

Those I have known who experience gender dysphoria often feel remarkably alone. They may experience something they do not understand ("Am I losing my mind?"), and if they choose to share that experience, they face the extraordinary challenge of explaining it to others. I try to assure them that they are not alone in the sense that I know and will not leave them, and I will work with them on finding others who can provide support. I also assure them that they are not alone in the sense that, while this is not a common experience, they are not the only person who has experienced gender dysphoria. I do want to know who else knows about the person's gender dysphoria, mostly because I want to develop some social support for the person as they navigate this terrain.

To help facilitate a discussion about disclosure to others, it can be helpful to provide psychoeducation on different types of constraints[9] that make disclosure difficult. These constraints essentially function as obstacles to disclosing to others. There are two types of constraints: proscriptive constraints and prescriptive constraints. *Proscriptive constraints* regarding gender identity communicate the following: "Discussions about gender identity are not welcome here." This message comes from individuals and communities for whom the topic is so threatening that there is no discussion to be had. This makes disclosure almost impossible for the person because the message is that the person's gender identity conflicts are not allowed to be talked about in this relationship or community. In contrast to proscriptive constraints, *prescriptive constraints* communicate the following: "Discussions about gender identity can and should be discussed, but we only discuss it in this certain way."[10] This can make discussing gender identity concerns difficult because the person who is struggling initially feels welcome to disclose but then is quickly told that there is only one way for them to actually think about their gender identity.

The person navigating gender identity concerns can begin to think about relationships and communities that subtly or not-so-subtly convey one or the other constraints. When such constraints are present, it is exceedingly difficult to disclose one's experience. Thinking through relationships and communities that reflect either of these constraints can help shorten the list of people to whom the person can disclose. Disclosure in this sense is an invitation to greater transparency and understanding of what the person has been facing.

Unfortunately, religious communities frequently struggle with coming alongside someone navigating gender identity concerns. If a person grows up in a religious community in which they received the message that a gender presentation that is not 100 percent male or 100 percent female is a sin, an abomination, this makes it all the more likely the person will keep what they are facing private and will continue to travel the road alone.

Some people who experience gender dysphoria find that telling another person is freeing because it means they are not alone in carrying that burden anymore. Others may feel incredibly anxious because they are certain that if they were to tell someone else, the other person's response would be rather negative, such as rejection, anger or hurt.

Sometimes distinguishing "how you are" from "who you are" may be helpful when sharing experiences of gender dysphoria with another person. I find this to be especially true when an adult shares with his or her parents. Now, if a person experienced early onset, the parents typically express concern and eventually bring their child in to see a professional who makes the diagnosis if warranted. If we are discussing late onset, this can be especially challenging, as it may go against how parents have always known and seen their child. One approach with parents might be to say something like this: "I think I am experiencing what is called gender dysphoria. It's like I have a strong sense within myself that doesn't match my body as a man (or as a woman) and I feel like someone more in-between. Can you tell me about how I behaved as a kid?"[11]

This approach allows the parents to discuss their memories of the person as a child, especially their memories of the person's gender-typical and gender-atypical behaviors. These are the parent's memories, and not the person's memories, but this approach may help bring parents in—to help parents invest a little more emotionally, and it shows them the person's desire to have them join him or her in the journey.

I also tell those who experience gender dysphoria that if the person they tell reacts with anger, disbelief, rejection or hurt after they tell them about their experiences, it is not their fault. I usually reiterate that they did not choose to experience gender dysphoria; they found themselves experiencing gender dysphoria, and this is not an issue of blaming but of realizing there may be negative reactions for different reasons.

Here are a few examples:

- Some religious leaders may react with anger, hurt and frustration because they are simply overwhelmed by something they do not understand or do not wish to investigate outside their religious doctrines.

- Some friends, family members or religious leaders may feel that if they are in any way supportive of people with gender dysphoria they are somehow denying the gospel or the truth. That is, "if you don't correct the sinner, you're complicit in the sin."

- Some parents may grieve what they believe is the loss of a dream, or perhaps several dreams. Maybe it is the loss of a dream that you, their child, would be married and that you would have the chance to feel what they've felt as parents. They may also be grieving because they are afraid they have not done enough for you as parents and have failed you in some way.

- Some grandparents may grieve the loss of what they believe is hope for a grandchild, which would fulfill their roles as grandparents.

- Some friends may be frightened that you may not be the outward person they have always known or may feel like you have been lying to them and react with gossip or scolding.[12]

IMPROVING COMMUNICATION

I mentioned in chapter two that people in the same family who love and support one another or who may be in conflict with one another frequently draw on different explanatory frameworks. These frameworks function as lenses or ways of seeing gender dysphoria. The three frameworks we have been discussing are the integrity framework, the disability framework and the diversity framework.

The example I gave was Jazz, a male-to-female gender dysphoric pre-adolescent who adopted a cross-gender identification as female. When asked, her preferred language was a diversity framework. She shared that she thought of being transgender as "special" or "unique." In contrast, her older sister used more of a disability framework to explain gender dysphoria to her friends: "I tell people that it's a disorder and that it wasn't . . . that it's not by choice." You could imagine yet another person in the community utilizing the integrity framework to question (from more of a religious faith perspective) whether cross-gender identification is the best option for a child.

To help improve communication, it can be useful to highlight the primary lens through which each person in the family sees the experience of gender dysphoria. Is a person seeing through a lens of diversity that speaks to identity, as Jazz was doing? Or is a person seeing through a lens of disability in order to marshal compassion from others, as Jazz's sister was doing? Or is still another person seeing through a lens of integrity that emphasizes sacredness in a way that may be part of the very same family or faith community? If so, just identifying the lens or framework is a first step in improving how they speak to one another by first helping them listen to each other, to come to a better understanding of each person's point of reference. Otherwise, family members and members of the same faith community will likely speak past one another.

MATTERS OF FAITH

In the study I conducted of male-to-female transgender Christians they noted conflicts with gender identity and religious identity in terms of personal faith, God and the local church.[13] Interestingly, some transgender Christians shared that their gender dysphoria led to a strengthening of their personal faith; others reported a past struggle with their faith, and still others left the organized religion with which they grew up. One sixty-two-year-old participant shared the following:

> Well, I've certainly been through the period(s?) of "Why Me, God?" And I've been through periods when I'd really liked to have attended worship services en femme.
>
> I've refrained from doing so, so as not to be disruptive of the spirit of reverence.[14]

Another fifty-eight-year-old participant shared perhaps an even more painful experience: "I am walking wounded, dry bones, defeated, tired of the struggle for normalcy or acceptance."[15]

For some, the challenges they faced brought them closer to God, but others reported a strained relationship with God because of their gender dysphoria. Particularly common was past conflict with the local church community or the persons and leaders who represent these organizations. One 57-year-old participant in the study noted above shared about an ongoing struggle with God:

> I shall work out my salvation with fear and trembling as I am in the process of being perfected. Either way I believe that God sees me through Christ and my hope is in His righteousness not my own. The biggest problem that I have in my relationship with Him is not reaching my own self-imposed standards, his Love never changes, I restrict how much of His Love I receive. But none the less I love Him with all my heart, if he asked me to stop dressing en-femme I would for Him, but unless he changed my transgendered condition Himself I would still be the same person I am.[16]

It seems to me that this is ultimately an important reference point: a person's relationship with God. As the church facilitates that relationship, a person navigating gender dysphoria will also be making important decisions about gender identity, expression and management of dysphoria. It is hard to say that there is one path or one resolution that is ultimately satisfying to everyone. All the while, a frequently asked question by those who are gender dysphoric is, "Does this mean I am going to hell?" If by this a person is referring to gender dysphoria, the answer is, "No, gender dysphoria does not separate you from God; it does not consign you to hell."

The path forward in the context of extreme gender dysphoria is difficult to identify. The topic often pulls otherwise thoughtful people to offer simple solutions in an attempt to live into a biblical sexual ethic, and it is the simplicity that may need to be thoughtfully and gently challenged:

> We can speak of the simple choice for or against God's new creation, the simple alternative of a broad way and a narrow way, the straightforward either-or opposition of sin and virtue. We can speak of the life of the believer as one in which there is love and no sin, and of the life of the unbeliever as one in which there is sin and no love.[17]

O'Donovan observes that these for/against categories are in part what it means to give morality meaning, to direct us eschatologically toward the purpose found in the "new creation."[18] So, yes, there is a moral reality and one that has been revealed to us and impressed upon us and our minds and bodies. However, this can quickly lead Christians to reduce complexity to simplicity by what O'Donovan sees as a legalism to a codified and comprehensive blueprint for moral action:

> [Legalism often produced in Christian ethics] attempts to ensure the simplicity of the concrete decision by making the codified law entirely comprehensive. If every eventuality can be foreseen and provided for in an elaboration of the moral code, then, when the moment of decision arrives, it is confronted in its simplest form as a choice for or against obeying God's law. The ambiguities have been cleared out of the way by the experts, so that the moral agent, provided that he will take expert advice, need not be troubled by the tasks of discernment but has only to take the simple decision of will seriously.[19]

As I indicated above, if there was ever a topic that elicited simplicity in the face of remarkable complexity, it is gender dysphoria. We are witnesses to simplicity in both the direction of conservatives who mock[20] those who experience gender dysphoria and attempt to resolve their dysphoria in some of the most invasive ways, as well as experts who may assume that transition to cross-gender identification is preferred with little thought given to the integrity and sacredness of sex in particular.

CONCLUDING THOUGHTS

A culture at war politically and over morality and epistemology contributes to reducing complexity to simplicity, from thoughtful reflection to media sound bites. Perhaps it is a miracle anyone is actually helped or ministered to in that context.

Yet the Christian enters into this discussion with a different reference point:

> The ultimate and simple decision is not found in the books of human deeds, but in the book of life, where it is a question of Yes or No: either a name is there, or it is not. But the book of life does not supplant the books of men's deeds; rather, those books, when read in the light of that book, take on the character of a correspondingly simple and final decision, a Yes or No to God's grace. However much our moral decisions strive for clarity, they are never unambiguous or translucent, even to ourselves. But—and is this not the gospel at the heart of evangelical ethics?—it is given to them by God's grace in Christ to add up to a final and unambiguous Yes, a work of love which will abide for eternity.[21]

In one of the first exchanges I had with a male-to-female transsexual Christian who I will refer to as Sara, she opened the exchange with, "I may have sinned in the decisions I made; I'm honestly not sure that I did the right thing. At the time, I felt excruciating distress. I thought I would take my life. I can't imagine going back. What would you have me do?"

That is a pretty disarming exchange. This is not someone who has made a commitment to a worldview and philosophy bent on deconstructing meaningful categories of sex and gender. If you had come to argue with Sara about a sexual ethic, you would not have found an opponent. She might have agreed with you, in fact. How does a person like Sara maintain a posture of repentance and a soft heart toward God in light of the impossible decisions she faced? Is there a Christian community that is willing to stand next to her in these impossible circumstances?

As a psychological condition, Gender Dysphoria is such a rare condition that we have little good research from which to draw strong conclusions. I have known people like Sara who experienced gender incongruence and a rise in the associated distress so strongly that they felt that nothing less than their sanity and their life were at stake. They desperately sought a resolution. This is not an argument that they then should pursue the most invasive procedures or cross-gender identification, but I also acknowledge that I understand and empathize with that decision, as painful as it often is.

Rather than reject the person facing such conflicts, the Christian community would do well to recognize the conflict and try to work with the person and with those who have expertise in this area to find the least invasive ways to manage the dysphoria and to offer compassion and mercy when that has not been possible. Perhaps future programs of research will provide greater insight and clarity into an area that seems particularly difficult to navigate at present. In the meantime, the Christian community can help foster growth in spiritual maturity among those who are facing impossible circumstances, as well as facilitate "a final and unambiguous Yes" to God's mercy and grace.

7

Toward a Christian Response

At the Level of the Institution

A LARGE CHRISTIAN UNIVERSITY IN CALIFORNIA was recently in the position to navigate the difficult terrain of gender identity concerns when a popular theology professor—Dr. Heather Ann Clements—shared his experience of coming to terms with gender identity questions he had been facing for some time. He shared that he preferred to be known as Heath Adam Ackley (or H. Adam Ackley).

According to news reports,[1] Adam came to terms with his transgender identity shortly after the publication of the *DSM-5*, which had changed the name "Gender Identity Disorder" to "Gender Dysphoria":

> You can't change someone's gender by giving them psychiatric medication. If they're born transgender, they're always going to be transgender. . . . APA has finally realized that . . . so I was taken off all the psych meds at the beginning of this year. I was told I am sane, and that I am a guy—I'm just a transgendered guy. And that's all I had to hear.

A few years prior to this report, Julie Nemecek (formerly John) settled a dispute with a small Christian college in Michigan following a complaint she filed with the US Equal Employment Opportunity Commission.[2]

More recently, a complaint was filed against a Christian university by a female-to-male transgender student who had requested on-campus male housing. News reports at the time suggested the student was offered single-room on-campus housing (or off-campus housing with males) but was denied on-campus male housing.[3]

I raise these examples to point out that the Christian community faces several challenges at present and will continue to face these challenges and more in the years to come surrounding gender identity, gender dysphoria and transgender issues. These examples are institutional tensions, but they also represent real people who were navigating gender identity concerns in the context of a Christian community. The Christian community and its institutions (churches, faith-based higher education, private schools, campgrounds, ministries and so on) will see more of these points of tensions in the years ahead.

It is important to realize that, in cases like these, if a person were to go to a mental health professional today and meet existing diagnostic criteria, they would likely be diagnosed with Gender Dysphoria. As an adult, they would hear about strategies for living into one's cross-gender identification. If that were male-to-female, for example, the person would consider hair removal, voice/vocal training, cross-dressing part time or full time, and options would also include hormonal treatment and sex-reassignment surgery. Such procedures might not be indicated, and not everyone who may qualify for hormones and surgery will make the decision to pursue them. Or they might do some surgical options but not many or not all of the options that are before them.

There are also children and adolescents who are faced with gender identity conflicts of one kind or another. It is an extremely rare presentation, but it is one with great sociocultural significant today, and most Christians and Christian communities are simply not prepared to have a thoughtful discussion around it. What is the best way to proceed?[4]

Let me say at the outset that there is no one way that will satisfy the number of stakeholders in these discussions—even not thinking of the broader culture but just the Christian community. Let me start by mapping out different experiences within the transgender community that have to be taken into consideration when Christians think about the best way to relate.

RELATING TO THE TRANSGENDER COMMUNITY

When Christians think about the transgender community, it may be helpful to recognize the range of ways in which transgender persons may relate to the church. There are going to be those who are unchurched or dechurched; there will be those who are traditionally believing Christians who are trying to navigate gender identity issues in their lives; and there will be those who are transgender and Christian but are navigating gender identity as essentially an expression of their preferred gender identity and have found identity and support within the LGBT community. Also, churches will want to think about how to respond to youth as well as adults in each of these areas. What if an adolescent describes him- or herself as genderfluid or otherwise engages in gender-bending behaviors in a way that suggests some questioning or experience of their gender identity being in flux?

In response to the unchurched and dechurched transgender community, the Christian community needs to ask what it will look like to be missional in the years to come. Keep in mind that this is a group that will be asking, "What does the church have to offer me?" The perception (and too often the reality) is that transgender persons who have nothing to do with the church perceive that the church would reject them out of hand. They have either had poor experiences with the church or they view the church as largely unimportant or irrelevant in their lives.

It has been observed that a traditional evangelical church focuses on behavior first, followed by belief in Christ and a sense of Christian community. It essentially looks like this:

Behave $\longrightarrow$ *Believe* $\longrightarrow$ *Belong*

This approach[5] begins with communicating expectations for change in how others behave. This may not be explicit, but it often has more to do with the comfort level of evangelicals who are sitting in the pews. They may believe the gospel is for those outside the church, but they do not want those outside the church to actually cross into the church until their behaviors change. What follows the expectation of behavior change is belief in Christ. Unfortunately, on the heels of the expectation of behavioral compliance, it can come across to those outside the church as, "Think the way we think," which is a hard message after the expectation to conform to behavioral norms. Then the message is: Now you belong. It is a remarkably conditional approach to the world, and one that, in my view, is not sustainable in our changing sociocultural context.

A missional church model offers a different outline:

Belong $\longrightarrow$ *Believe* $\longrightarrow$ *Become*

A missional church[6] focuses on first being in relationship (*belong*) then moves toward an opportunity to live one's testimony to an unbelieving culture (*believe*). Only when a person enters into that relationship is there any thought given to who a person becomes over time as they grow in their relationship with Christ (*become*). Some people will insert the word *behave* where I have *become*, but I prefer the designation *become* to *behave*, as it reminds evangelicals that the process of sanctification is not a checklist of behaviors but a dynamic process of growing in Christlikeness.

What does "become" look like? It is difficult to say. Although some people who experience gender dysphoria along a continuum may be able to live into their birth sex, some are not able to. Their dysphoria is significant and sustained. For some, it has been life threatening. Some people will manage their gender dysphoria through various, creative ways, and I encourage the least-invasive steps if possible. Still others may elect more invasive steps in keeping with current mental and medical health options and recommendations. Perhaps these steps will be seen more as pastoral accommodations (drawing more from the integrity and disability frameworks) rather than an affirmation, as seen in diversity framework.

But missional models of church are messy and much more complicated than many churches realize. Just the fact that there are multiple stakeholders in a church that considers following a missional model is often a tremendous challenge. Stakeholders include current members who range in age across multiple generations, and these cohorts bring with them different assumptions and attitudes that must be taken into account. In other words, people who have been comfortable in church will not be comfortable in church. And every missional church I have met with faces difficult decisions on where to draw the line that has to do with community standards for things like Communion or the Lord's Supper (is it an open table or a closed table?), service to others (e.g., greeter, parking attendant), childcare, teaching, leading small groups and leadership (e.g., elder, deacon). Even the message of belonging can be lost when a person wants to serve—let's say as a greeter—but is transgender and others in the church raise concerns about what message is being sent to the community.

Also, it should not be assumed that greater Christlikeness is the same as having experiences of gender dysphoria abate. Rather, many people who know and love Christ have besetting conditions that have simply not resolved as a result of their belief in Christ as their Savior. Indeed, it may very well be that it is in the context of these enduring conditions that God brings about greater Christlikeness.

ON DRAWING LINES

One church I consulted with wanted to discuss at what point church discipline takes place. We expanded the discussion beyond gender atypical presentations to a broader vision for shepherding believers in the local church. The leadership was thinking that they tend to draw a line for behavioral expectations of those who attend their church at membership, which the leadership saw as a clear indication a person was willing to sit under the teaching and shepherding influence of the church pastor and elders. As we discussed the idea further, however, they talked about how they allowed nonmembers to serve in several capacities, such as greeters and parking attendants. When they thought together how they would respond to a male-to-female transgender person who was not a member and wished to be a greeter, they acknowledged they had not thought through the complexities of the situation and had a difficult time coming up with a response, let alone a shared understanding of what they should expect from a person who wished to serve in that capacity. It is one of the challenges that comes up with drawing lines and having a clear idea who is making a mature and educated decision to sit under the leadership of the local church. These challenges include recognizing what that means to the person seeking membership and to those in leadership, as well as how to relate spiritual leadership to various issues that might arise in a cultural context in which cross-gender identification as one way of managing dysphoria or expressing oneself is and will be increasingly supported by medical and mental health professionals.

One woman I know who is a Christian and transgender likens this to the watchful waiting approach with a child who displays symptoms of gender dysphoria. For her, a new Christian is a spiritual child in Christ who is beginning a journey in terms of how that person's faith shapes their experience of their gender identity questions and where they might go from where they are today. This would likely be experienced by a transgender person who is new to Christianity as quite gracious and supportive.

In discussions about people who are navigating gender identity issues, there will likely be disagreement as to what "become" looks like for the transgender person, in part because of different explanatory frameworks (integrity, disability and diversity frameworks). But what we can agree on is that helping a person grow in greater spiritual maturity brings that maturity to the decision-making process in a spirit of humility.

As the church thinks about transgender persons who are Christians and trying to navigate gender identity issues in keeping with their biological sex with an emphasis on managing their dysphoria in the least invasive way, we would do well to recognize how this approach often reflects the integrity framework and the disability framework, both of which see the phenomenon as a reflection of a fallen world. The emphasis in the disability framework is that, as a disability, it is not a reflection of personal sin but more a question of how to manage the dysphoria itself. What is missing here, however, is what is so helpful from the diversity framework.

Recall that the diversity framework provides messages about identity and community that provide that person with a genuinely meaningful sense of self and kinship that is not frequently experienced in the local church. This should help the local church grow in their empathy and compassion and give greater thought to how to be family—how to provide a kinship network—to the person who is navigating these concerns. When we fail to meet these needs, we essentially drive the person back to another message about self and other, about identity and community. Are Christians prepared to enter into a sustained relationship with someone who experiences gender dysphoria? Are Christians prepared to do so without the condition that the person manages that dysphoria in a way the Christian community would support? This will get complicated and messy, but are Christians prepared to communicate "We're in this together" and "I'm with you on this journey"?

When we think about transgender persons who identify as Christian but are navigating their gender identity primarily as an expression of their felt gender identity and have found an identity and support within the LGBT community, we would do well to recognize ways in which "transgender" can function as a way of exercising resilience in response to marginalization and pain. Their identity as transgender and the view that they are expressing their true self has clearly provided a path through which they can find hope and life, and that may indeed contrast sharply with what they have found in the church.

What such an approach may not account for as well is what we find in the integrity and disability frameworks. These frameworks give us pause about movements away from biological sex and a gender binary, at least as anchor points for our understanding of creation norms. However, these frameworks can be held with humility, recognizing that we do not want to artificially endorse rigid gender stereotypes that make cultural normative expression of gender roles a marker of obedience to God or something along those lines. The disability framework provides another reference point that might underscore managing dysphoria rather than focusing on expression of the true self as such. This would not be held out as an expectation to the person but as an opportunity for exploration and consideration in the context of a sustained relationship with that person.

We can see that these three broad experiences within the transgender community draw forth very different responses. Different experiences of gender identity concerns will require different responses, so it takes time and discernment to understand how to proceed.

CARE AND COMPASSION IN THE BODY OF CHRIST

A young person walked through the side doors of the large church and into the hall where the youth group was about to meet for an evening event. This particular youth—a male, everyone would later say—was in clothing that was difficult to identify as belonging to either a guy or a girl; pretty androgynous clothing in hindsight. The youth pastor saw him enter and made a point to engage him. He walked right up to the teen and extended a warm greeting and engaged him in conversation for a minute or two. However, the youth pastor was called away; he had to attend to other details before the start of the evening meeting. He was away for no more than a few minutes, but it was during that time that three other kids from the youth group spoke to the visitor and things deteriorated quickly. Their focus was on his outfit; the perception that he was genderfluid in ways that went against local, conventional gender norms. They spoke to him about the ways guys are to dress, about what it means to be a guy and a follower of Christ. As you might imagine, the teen was long gone before the youth pastor knew what had happened.

In a study of transgender Christians, participants were asked about their experience with Christian faith communities. One male-to-female transgender Christian shared an exchange with a previous pastor:

> I once explained to a pastor in a previous church my transgender situation and he rejected me totally. He said it was something that he could not cope with, so I have kept quiet about it ever since in subsequent churches as I would not wish to hurt those who cannot cope with who I am.[7]

To provide effective support today, there is a need for the church to be able to cope with the disclosure of gender dysphoria among those who experience it and have the courage to share what they are going through.

In light of these stories and dozens more I could share, it may be helpful in ministry to reflect on contrasting terms of inclusion from the transgender community and the Christian community. This helps the Christian community think about messages that are being sent, helps us scrutinize those messages, and helps us identify other messages we may want to convey.

TERMS OF INCLUSION

The terms of inclusion for those who are navigating gender incongruence might be understood in the context of what has been referred to as identity politics. As Heyes observes,

> Identity politics starts from analyses of oppression to recommend, variously, the reclaiming, redescription, or transformation of previously stigmatized accounts of group membership. Rather than accepting the negative scripts offered by a dominant culture about one's own inferiority, one transforms one's own sense of self and community, often through consciousness-raising.[8]

My observation has been that the terms of inclusion from the transgender community are not as rigid as in other communities. In some regards you might say that the term is the embrace of a transgender identity and being a part of the transgender community. But I have not seen this focus on identity organized in quite the same way ("around a single axis") as it might be with other minorities:

> To the extent that identity politics urges mobilization around a single axis, it will put pressure on participants to identify that axis as their defining feature, when in fact they may well understand themselves as integrated selves who cannot be represented so selectively or even reductively (Spelman 1988). The second form of essentialism is closely related to the first: generalizations made about particular social groups in the context of identity politics may come to have a disciplinary function within the group, not just describing but also dictating the self-understanding that its members should have.[9]

However, the range of experiences within the transgender community— the many ways in which gender is experienced and expressed, as well as private versus public expression—has meant there is no single axis; subsequently, there is great support for one another and for the many ways in which transgender people sort out gender identity issues and either manage dysphoria or express themselves. So the acceptance within the community is rather broad, in my experience, and it is important to keep in mind that the acceptance a person experiences there gives that person a much-needed sense of identity and community.

The terms of inclusion from the local church are that a person fit into the male-female binary and experience congruence between biological or birth sex and psychological and emotional experience of gender identity. To differing degrees in different settings, there can be more or less rigid stereotypes for gender roles and norms that may make gender identity conflicts that much more challenging.

Although there are multiple paths in front of any one person whose gender dysphoria rises to the level of significant distress or impairment, each person is going to benefit from a supportive community and related resources.

Mike was born biologically male. He has been a Christian essentially all of his life. He experienced some gender incongruence as a child but believed it had largely resolved by adolescence and certainly by the time he married his high school sweetheart. The experience of gender incongruence reemerged later in his middle adulthood. In his attempts to either manage that dysphoria or express his sense of self, his church community was unable to create an atmosphere of support for him and his family. He was confronted for how he had grown out his hair and his choice of more gender-ambiguous apparel. To make a long story short, he was not compliant with the church leadership's expectations for his appearance, which he experienced as narrow and rigid in terms of gender stereotypes, and he was removed from his leadership role and essentially dis-fellowshipped from the faith community.

There are two sides to every story. I do not know all of the details about Mike's experience and how it was or should have been handled, but it raises questions we all have to grapple with in terms of how to respond to gender identity concerns in the context of a faith community.

I shared in chapter five that an estimated 50 percent of people who meet criteria for and receive services for Gender Dysphoria drop out, likely due to frustration with the process or possibly other reasons. The paths that are before them include (1) resolving their Gender Dysphoria in accordance with their biological sex; (2) engaging in cross-dressing behavior intermittently to manage dysphoria; or (3) adopt the cross-gender role, which may or may not include hormonal treatment and sex-reassignment surgery.[10]

In each case, as a person navigates gender incongruence in adulthood, whether they resolve their dysphoria in accordance with their birth sex, engage in cross-dressing behavior intermittently, or adopt a cross-gender role, they will have common concerns and areas of need moving forward. Each will need social support, assistance with and from family members, help in exploring their personal faith, aid in finding a corporate faith community, assistance in learning and applying helpful coping activities, and so much more.

Table 7.1. Pathways in Adulthood and Issues with Support

Path 1	Path 2	Path 3	Path 4
Unresolved outcome.	Resolve in accordance with their birth sex.	Engage in cross-dressing behavior and role intermittently (often privately or in distant venues/locales).	Adopt cross-gender role and identity, which may include hormonal treatment and sex-reassignment surgery.

Social support, family relationships, personal faith, corporate faith community, healthy coping activities, address any co-occurring mental health issues, and so on.

I imagine some readers will be thinking to themselves, *I just want the person to choose the right path.* I can understand that thought. However, paths are chosen with reference to a number of factors, not in isolation. People choose paths in the context of the community they have been able to form around themselves. If you want a person to choose a path that seems more redemptive, you will want to be part of a redemptive community that facilitates that kind of decision making for every person who is a member. Recall, though, that redemption frequently takes the form of making meaning out of suffering. With gender dysphoria, there is meaning to be found in one's gender identity and in the state of tension experienced in gender dysphoria.

A REDEMPTIVE COMMUNITY

I opened the section on "Care and Compassion in the Body of Christ" with a story about a young person who left a youth group despite the youth pastor's attempts to demonstrate hospitality. I want to acknowledge that the story about the youth pastor raises additional questions about what it means to be a redemptive community, particularly the corporate/communal aspect of attempts at inclusion. When teens in a youth group can drive a young person away from a church that is intentional about reaching out to those on the margins, it has to at least raise the question of whether youth are able to understand the nuanced messages of inclusivity and tolerance while also holding biblical perspectives on complex matters.

I see two common impulses that the church may need to re-evaluate. One impulse is to convey the integrity framework to the exclusion of the potential benefits seen in the disability or diversity frameworks. Such a church would be of little relevance to people within their own community who are navigating gender identity concerns, nor would they have much of a way of communicating and understanding concerns about identity and community that are increasingly relevant to the broader culture. I imagine the thinking would be something along these lines: "The best witness to the culture is orthodoxy around a biblical understanding of sex and gender." However, as I have suggested, too often Christians can fall into more rigid stereotypes about gender that reflect more cultural concerns than biblical concerns, and people can overcorrect toward stereotypes out of concern for the deconstruction of sex/gender norms. In my view, such a church may struggle with compassion and empathy and provide little by way of a sense of identity and care to those within their own community who may be navigating gender identity concerns, let alone be able to understand the experiences and interests of those who are in their local community. Beyond that, we are going to see increasing numbers of people within the culture who are not likely to understand the foundations to the integrity framework and who may experience the church as having no regard for fundamental interests (identity/community) that are best met through the diversity framework.

The other impulse is to convey tolerance and inclusivity—to draw exclusively on the diversity framework to the neglect of the integrity and disability frameworks. We can imagine a church that is so focused on cultural relevance it loses sight of the ways in which some are pushing hard to deconstruct sex and gender norms. Churches with this emphasis face the challenge of becoming a welcoming place at the risk of conveying to youth who are on their own developmental journey that there is little by way of relevance to a Christian view of sex and gender and what it means to be a part of a Christian community.

Some readers will likely be thinking: *But that's exactly what we want to teach—all are welcome!* My point is that the nuance we are discussing requires a fairly sophisticated understanding of complex issues, and the trade-off may lead many young Christians to lose any sense of biblical absolutes when little can be said about things like sex differences and gender. We need good examples of what a church looks like that models and lives out a balance of welcoming and ministry with clear biblical testimony.

These two inclinations I have described may represent two different ways in which churches are missional. The first one we do not tend to think about as missional, but I believe a case can be made that such a church is attempting to be *inwardly missional* with its focus on clear teachings for those who are within the community. This kind of church places greater emphasis on the integrity framework. It is a church that sees as its mission the communication of a faithful, biblical witness about sexuality and gender to those who reside within. Such a church may risk not being as hospitable to those on the outside (not being outwardly directed, which is a more common understanding of a missional church) because the emphasis is on conveying biblical truths to those on the inside.

The other way of being missional is what I think of as *outwardly missional*, by which I mean the focus is on being missional to the local, broader community in the area surrounding the church itself. The emphasis is on reaching out, inviting in and creating a sense of belonging, as I indicated above. People are frequently drawn to this model because so many apparent obstacles to being a part of a church are removed. The risk here is that in making every effort to be inclusive, people in the church may actually experience some confusion about identifying biblical standards and being a biblical witness. This is especially challenging in the example I cited above in which we are counting on young Christians who are on their own journey to grapple with a rather complex and nuanced understanding of sex and gender that may be hard to fully understand.

Also, as we move forward in creating redemptive communities for all Christians, including those who are navigating gender identity concerns, we have to acknowledge the sociocultural context in which we live and in which the person is making these decisions. The prevailing view within the mental health field is to address the dysphoria through cross-gender identification and expression, supported in the context of therapy, and with the possibility of additional steps to facilitate a transition. That decision is being made in a sociocultural context in which the cultural trajectory is toward the absence of (or deconstruction of) gender norms and distinctives. The Christian community can uphold differences in biological sex and gender norms but will want to do so while also resisting rigid gender stereotyping that frequently functions as a knee-jerk response to this cultural momentum.

Based on my consultations with many churches throughout the United States, I do not think there is one blueprint that every church can follow to be that kind of redemptive community. I encourage churches that are either inwardly or outwardly missional to at least recognize the strengths and also the potential shortcomings to one or the other approach, as they may benefit from offsetting some of the weaknesses in their approach with more intentional steps in light of our overarching discussion. Toward that end, there are some concepts that may be helpful to the Christian community that wants to create redemptive space. These are clarity, relational ethic, humility, climate, sanctification and social support.

Clarity. The issue of clarity has to do with thoughtful reflection on a biblical perspective of concepts like sex and gender. What do we teach and affirm about sex and gender? As the church wrestles with how to provide appropriate care to those in our communities who are navigating gender identity concerns, we would be wise to remember that good theology and sensitive pastoral care must be reflected in the doctrine, policies, and pastoral applications of the local church. As we sort out good scholarship in this area and how to communicate it and apply it in ministry and pastoral care, we do well to keep in view that the very nature of sex and gender is being deconstructed by some people in these discussions in ways that even many transgender persons would be uncomfortable with.

Relational ethic. As I noted earlier, there is reason to believe that the next generation of Christians—even in cases in which they retain a traditional Christian sexual ethic—places greater emphasis on sustained relationships with those with whom they disagree. Because churches are comprised of Christians from multiple generations, there may at times be tensions between those who value a relational ethic and those who do not. In my view, thoughtful teaching on sexuality and gender will have to take that into consideration as we consider how to value others, form relationships in a diverse and pluralistic culture, and sustain those relationships while living faithfully before God.

Humility. The church could demonstrate greater humility about what we know and do not know about the topic of gender dysphoria. Even as the Christian community offers clarity in articulating a biblical witness about important constructs in this area, we can still be humble stewards of what we know and what we do not know. It would be helpful if scientists and others who are stakeholders in these discussions were also demonstrating humility, but we can do what we can within our own communities to consider the current limitations to our understanding in this area at this time.

Pastors or other Christian leaders can also demonstrate humility by being a resource to a multidisciplinary treatment team. I would not want a pastor to reach the conclusion that reading this book now qualifies them to treat someone who is gender dysphoric. As I have shared, if a person's gender dysphoria reaches a level at which that person receives the diagnosis of Gender Dysphoria, he or she may receive input from various mental health professionals, some with expertise in gender identity issues, as well as medical personnel, such as endocrinologists. Humility can be seen in being a part of a larger team with different perspectives but with a common goal of serving the best interest of the person who is requesting help.

Climate. I return to the question of rigid gender stereotypes. Many men's ministries focus on themes of biblical manhood but end up looking too much like cultural associations with masculinity that are likely to be very difficult for the person struggling with gender identity concerns. Similarly, women's ministries can focus on a kind of cultural femininity that is portrayed as the biblical expression of being a woman. In other words, too often, in response to assertions that appear to seek to deconstruct sex and gender, Christians respond not with a dispassionate reflection on the view but with a knee-jerk reaction that swings the pole in the other direction.

There are other practical steps that could improve climate. One female-to-male transgender Christian shared, "One thing I have learned is that no matter how compassionate the people and pastor are, if there isn't a family bathroom, things get complicated fast and you don't go back." These may seem like small things, but they are practical steps that can have a big impact.

Sanctification. Christians walk out their faith in a relationship with Christ and as a result of the Holy Spirit in a way that is meant to move them toward greater Christlikeness. This is sanctification, or being set apart for God's purposes. It refers to being made holy. The way I tend to think about sanctification is growing in spiritual maturity. Spiritual maturity informs decision making. In an atmosphere of grace, can the Christian community invite one another to greater spiritual maturity to inform important decisions that are often down the road? This is a long process that requires from all of us a lot of space, grace and patience. It is important to provide a kind of sustained presence (out of our own developing spiritual maturity, which will certainly be challenged in this complex arena) while someone is navigating gender identity concerns, meeting with experts in gender identity issues and making key decisions about how best to manage their experiences of gender dysphoria.

Social support. With the other things in place—clarity, humility, improved climate and an emphasis on personal sanctification—we are now in a position to offer the kind of social support that is so needed today. In an atmosphere of grace, can we come alongside people who are navigating this difficult terrain? What I envision here is a small community of fellow believers who are willing to pray for and with the person navigating this terrain, as well as to identify and follow through on practical needs that can be met in the life of the person who is gender dysphoric.

CONCLUDING THOUGHTS

I opened this chapter with several examples at Christian institutions that represent the conflicts the Christian community is heading toward. On matters of sex and gender, and in our increasingly diverse and pluralistic culture, a traditional Christian perspective on these matters will continue to be challenged in many settings and for a range of reasons. We will be witness to legal challenges to the way in which Christians have historically related to these topics, and that may put many Christians in greater conflict with the broader culture. Based on the consultations I have provided over the years, these will be issues at Christian campgrounds, faith-based institutions of higher education, churches, not-for-profit entities that provide humanitarian relief worldwide, and many other institutions. This will be in the area of employee hiring, health care provisions, lodging and facilities, and much more.

The Christian community has several ongoing responsibilities moving forward. These have to do with thoughtful scholarship in this area, which includes:

1. critical analysis and engagement with the work being done in the area of sex and gender

2. thoughtful engagement with best practices in clinical service provision to those who have been diagnosed with Gender Dysphoria

3. listening to the experiences of faithful believers who are navigating gender identity conflicts in their own lives

4. identifying the best way to be a faithful witness to a broader culture in which norms regarding sex and gender are eroding

5. engaging with "convicted civility" those who are actively deconstructing norms related to both sex and gender

6. identifying and implementing best practices as the body of Christ and, in particular, the local church in relation to unchurched and dechurched transgender persons

7. providing sensitive pastoral care to those in the Body of Christ who are navigating this terrain

This book is one modest step in this direction. I do not think Christians will speak with one voice on the topics of gender dysphoria and gender variant presentations. As I shared previously, the topic of gender dysphoria is not the same as homosexuality. The question of applying a Christian sexual ethic to same-sex behavior appears clearer to many Christians—although this is also being disputed in many settings, particularly mainline denominations and among younger Christians.

I have made the case that evangelical Christians may benefit from an integrated framework that can provide a way to respond to the different challenges the Christian community is facing. That integrated framework is based on the three existing lenses through which people often approach the topic of gender identity and gender dysphoria: the integrity framework, the disability framework and the diversity framework. Evangelical Christians are understandably drawn first and foremost to the integrity framework with its emphasis on the sacredness and essential elements of maleness and femaleness. As I have pointed out, evangelicals will be cautious about the disability framework and likely quite critical of the diversity framework. However, in my view, each of the three frameworks may provide important considerations that, taken together, inform a thoughtful, reasoned Christian response to gender identity and gender dysphoria. As we look at the broader cultural discussions and the challenges facing Christian institutions, it is important to realize how speaking solely with reference to the integrity framework will increasingly isolate evangelicals from a cultural context in which the diversity framework is emerging as most salient and is frequently a source of guidance within the mental health professions, which draw principally on the diversity framework and, to a lesser extent, the disability framework.

The way forward is to clearly identify which framework is the point of reference to those with whom you are in dialogue. Among those who advance the diversity framework, keep in mind the differences between strong forms of that framework (with the goal of deconstructing both sex and gender norms) and weak forms (that are primarily concerned with identity and community). As the church learns from each of the three frameworks, we begin to have an integrated framework that informs both ministry settings and Christian engagement with the broader culture. Christians can benefit from valuing and speaking into the sacredness found in the integrity framework, the compassion we witness in the disability framework, and the identity and community considerations we see in the diversity framework. No one framework in isolation will provide a sufficient response or a comprehensive Christian model of pastoral care or cultural engagement.

Notes

CHAPTER 1: GENDER IDENTITY, GENDER DYSPHORIA AND APPRECIATING COMPLEXITY

[1]I first recounted this story in Mark A. Yarhouse and Erica S. N. Tan, *Sexuality and Sex Therapy: A Comprehensive Christian Appraisal* (Downers Grove, IL: InterVarsity Press Academic, 2014), pp. 318-19. The extended account is from Christine Jorgensen's autobiography, *Christine Jorgensen: A Personal Autobiography* (San Francisco: Cleis Press, 1967).

[2]American Psychiatric Association, *Diagnostic and Statistical Manual of Mental Disorders*, 5th ed. (Washington, DC: American Psychiatric Publishing, 2013), pp. 451-59.

[3]Throughout this book I will cite research on Gender Dysphoria and what used to be referred to as Gender Identity Disorder. So as not to confuse the reader, I will use "Gender Dysphoria" for consistency and flow, even in cases in which I am referring to a study that used "Gender Identity Disorder." These are not identical diagnoses, as the criteria changed in 2013 with the publication of *DSM-5*. If it is important to make the distinction, I will reference the diagnostic terms used at the time of the study.

[4]The original report presented Jazz at age six, among other gender dysphoric youth (https://www.youtube.com/watch?v=YfqmEYC_rMI). Walters provided an update on Jazz at age eleven: https://www.youtube.com/watch?v=bJw3s85EcxM.

[5]Stanton L. Jones, "Is Sex or Gender a Choice?," in forthcoming *Holman Worldview Study Bible*.

[6]Other terms sometimes used for intersex conditions include "ambiguous genitalia," "disorders of sex development," and "male and female pseudohermaphroditism." Tom Mazur, Melissa Colsman and David E. Sandberg, "Intersex: Definition, Examples, Gender Stability and the Case Against Merging with Transsexualism," in *Principles of Transgender Medicine and Surgery*, ed. Randi Ettner, Stan Monstrey and A. Evan Eyler (New York: Hayworth Press, 2007), p. 236.

[7]Turner Syndrome is another genetic disorder of gonadal differentiation that "is the consequence of a chromosomal genetic abnormality in females characterized by a missing or partially deleted X chromosome." Ibid., p. 241.

[8]True hermaphroditism is defined "by the presence of both testicular and ovarian tissue in the same individual" and is "associated with a number of chromosomal patterns: 46XX (most common), combined 46XX/46XY chimerism, or 46XY (rare)." Ibid., p. 242.

[9]American Psychiatric Association, *Diagnostic and Statistical Manual*, pp. 452-53.

[10]This term may be new to some readers. As defined here, cisgender (or just cis) references persons who are essentially not transgender or gender nonconforming. It comes from the contrast of trans (or "on the other side of"—think of taking a transatlantic flight from New York to London) with cis (which means "on this side of") (www.oxforddictionaries. com/us/definition/american_english/cis-). The view that there is a "system of oppression" with reference to cisgender persons is referred to by proponents as *cisgenderism*, a "system of oppression that privileges cisgender identities and experiences over TGNC [transgender and gender nonconforming] identities and experiences, or perpetuates prejudicial attitudes and discriminatory behaviors that result in ignoring, denigrating or stigmatizing TGNC people or any forms of behavior or gender expression that lie outside of the traditional gender binary." American Psychological Association's proposed *Guidelines for Psychological Practice with Transgender and Gender Non-Conforming Clients*, p. 5; temporarily posted at http://www.apa.org, retrieved May 27, 2014. Similarly, advocates of this view, which is steeped in queer theory and draws heavily on Michel Foucault and Judith Butler, argue that "cissexual privilege refers to the rights and social abilities of people whose gender identity matches their birth gender, many of which go unseen and unexamined." Kelby Harrison, *Sexual Deceit: The Ethics of Passing* (Lanham, MD: Lexington Books, 2013), p. 12.

[11]In a consensus statement on the management of intersex conditions, Peter Lee and colleagues discuss five major domains:

(1) gender assignment must be avoided before expert evaluation in newborns; (2) evaluation and long-term management must be performed at a center with an experienced multidisciplinary team; (3) all individuals should receive a gender assignment; (4) open communication with patients and families is essential, and participation in decision-making is encouraged; and (5) patient and family concerns should be respected and addressed in strict confidence.

Peter A. Lee, Christopher P. Houk, S. Faisal Ahmed and Ieuan A. Hughes, "Consensus Statement on Management of Intersex Disorders," *Pediatrics* 118, no. 2 (2006); updated online at http://pediatrics.aappublications.org/content/118/2/e488.full.html.

[12]David Kinnaman, of the Barna Group, is quoted in this online article: "America's Change of Mind on Same-Sex Marriage and LGBTQ Rights," Barna Group, July 13, 2013, https://www.barna.org/component/content/article/36-homepage-main-promo/618-barna -update-04-25-2013#.U48VuS_gWB4.

[13]Ibid.

[14]Jones, "Is Sex or Gender a Choice?"

[15]Mark A. Yarhouse and Trista L. Carr, "MtF Transgender Christians' Experiences: A Qualitative Study," *Journal of LGBT Issues in Counseling* 6, no. 1 (2012): 26.

[16]See Trista L. Carr and Mark A. Yarhouse, "God and the Transgender Person," in *Gender Identity: Disorders, Developmental Perspectives and Social Implications* (New York: Nova Science Publishers, in press).

CHAPTER 2: A CHRISTIAN PERSPECTIVE ON GENDER DYSPHORIA

[1]Milton J. Erickson, *Introducing Christian Doctrine*, 2nd ed. (Grand Rapids: Baker Books, 2001), p. 68.

[2]Ibid., p. 75.

[3]Judson Poling, "What Does the Bible Say About Gender?" meeting at Willow Creek Church, South Barrington, Illinois, February 22, 2014.

[4]For example, some theologians have treated transsexuality as an "extension of the issue of homosexuality." Robert A. J. Gagnon, "Transsexuality and Ordination" (2007): www .robgagnon.net/articles/TranssexualityOrdination.pdf.

[5]Complex questions also arise if a person transitions from, say, male to female and enters into a relationship with a man who is now attracted to her as a woman. As one colleague with expertise in this area observed, from the referent of birth sex, this is homosexual behavior. From the referent of gender identity, this will be heterosexual behavior as experienced by the male-to-female transgender person.

[6]One female-to-male transgender Christian who reviewed this book manuscript shared that having a diagnosis can add another layer of complication, as the diagnosis supports the legitimacy of the problem, which is important. But reducing gender dysphoria to a diagnosis left this person feeling trapped, as there seemed to be no spiritual solution.

[7]However, it has been noted that the "soft men" referred to in 1 Corinthians 6:9 were thought to have feminized "themselves in appearance and matter to attract male sex partners." Gagnon, "Transsexuality and Ordination," p. 5.

[8]Evangelical Alliance Policy Commission [EAPC], *Transsexuality: A Report of the Evangelical Alliance Policy Commission* (Reading, UK: Cox & Wyman, 2000), p. 45.

[9]Ibid., p. 46.

[10]Ibid.

[11]Ibid., p. 47.

[12]Ibid.

[13]Ibid.

[14]Adrian Thatcher, *God, Sex and Gender: An Introduction* (West Sussex, UK: Wiley-Blackwell, 2011), p. 147.

[15]Poling, "What Does the Bible Say About Gender?" p. 2.

[16]Thatcher, *God, Sex and Gender*, p. 148.

[17]Ibid.

[18]In discussing the cultural context of the Ancient Israelites or, for that matter, the first-century church, I am not suggesting that there is too much hermeneutical distance between the first century and the twenty-first century, nor that the recorded history has no relevance for Christians today. I am concerned that just such a mistake is made by some authors who have attempted to develop exegetical models that work far too hard to move the reader away from the plain reading of Scripture.

[19]Heather Looy and Hessel Bouma III, "The Nature of Gender: Gender Identity in Persons Who Are Intersexed or Transgendered," *Journal of Psychology and Theology* 33, no. 3 (2005), 166-78.

[20]Ibid., p. 176.

[21]Stanton L. Jones, "Sexuality," in *Baker Encyclopedia of Psychology and Counseling*, D. G. Benner and P. C. Hill (Grand Rapids: Baker, 1999), p. 1107.

[22]Ibid.

[23]Ibid.

[24]Ibid., pp. 1107-13.

[25]Poling, "What Does the Bible Say About Gender?" p. 2.

[26]Madhur Ingalhalikur, "Sex Differences in the Structural Connectome of the Human Brain," *Proceedings of the National Academy of the Sciences* 11, no. 2 (2013): www.pnas.org /content/early/2013/11/27/1316909110.

[27]Looy and Bouma, "The Nature of Gender," p. 174.

[28]Ibid., p. 174.

[29]Christopher Chenault Roberts, *Creation and Covenant: The Significance of Sexual Difference in the Moral Theology of Marriage* (New York: T & T Clark, 2007), p. 225.

[30]Ibid., p. 226.

[31]Heather Looy, "Male and Female God Created Them: The Challenge of Intersexuality," *Journal of Psychology and Christianity* 21, no. 1 (2002): 17.

[32]Tom Mazur, Melissa Colsman and David E. Sandberg, "Intersex: Definition, Examples, Gender Stability and the Case Against Merging with Transsexualism," in *Principles of Transgender Medicine and Surgery*, ed. Randi Ettner, Stan Monstrey and A. Evan Eyler (New York: Hayworth Press, 2007), p. 242.

[33]Stanton L. Jones, "Is Sex or Gender a Choice?," in forthcoming *Holman Worldview Study Bible*.

[34]Ibid.

[35]See http://eve-tushnet.blogspot.com/2010_06_01_archive.html#1921445070183139.

[36]See Mark A. Yarhouse, *Understanding Sexual Identity: A Resource for Youth Ministry* (Grand Rapids: Zondervan, 2013), pp. 27-28.

[37]Oliver O'Donovan, *Resurrection and Moral Order: An Outline for Evangelical Ethics*, 2nd ed. (Grand Rapids: Eerdmans, 1994), p. 19.

[38]Looy and Bouma, "The Nature of Gender," p. 166.

[39]For a discussion of the purposes of sexuality, such as procreative, unitive and instructive,

see Mark A. Yarhouse and Erica S. N. Tan, *Sexuality and Sex Therapy: A Comprehensive Christian Appraisal* (Downers Grove, IL: IVP Academic, 2014), pp. 34-36.

[40]Richard Mouw, *Uncommon Decency: Christian Civility in an Uncivil World* (Downers Grove, IL: InterVarsity Press, 2010). Drawing upon Martin Marty, Richard Mouw discusses the importance of Christians displaying convicted civility. His concern is that there are too many Christians who are strong on expressing convictions but weak on displaying civility. Likewise, there are too many Christians who are remarkably civil, yet others know very little about what they believe or hold convictions about.

[41]O'Donovan, *Resurrection and Moral Order*, p. 52.

[42]Poling, "What Does the Bible Say About Gender?" p. 5.

[43]O'Donovan, *Resurrection and Moral Order*, p. 70.

[44]Ibid., p. 5.

[45]Roberts, *Creation and Covenant*, p. 7.

[46]Ibid., p. 8.

[47]Ibid. Beth Felker Jones offers a thoughtful reflection on the resurrection of the body as relevant to the gospel. She argues that the "bodily resurrection is not peripheral to the Christian gospel. In fact, it is determinative of any theological attempt to rightly conceive not only human bodies as created, but also human persons as redeemed." Later she writes, "Our bodies now must refer to the resurrection bodies to come. The doctrine of the bodily resurrection points us to a way of conceiving our whole selves, body and soul, as ordered toward God." Beth Felker Jones, *Marks of His Wounds: Gender Politics and Bodily Resurrection* (New York: Oxford University Press, 2007), pp. 113-14.

[48]O'Donovan, *Resurrection and Moral Order*, p. 247.

[49]Gagnon, "Transsexuality and Ordination," www.robgagnon.net/articles/Transsexuality Ordination.pdf.

[50]Ibid., p. 3.

[51]Ibid., p. 4.

[52]Looy and Bouma, "The Nature of Gender," p. 176.

[53]Heather Looy, "Sex Differences: Evolved, Constructed and Designed," *Journal of Psychology and Theology* 29, no. 4 (2001): 311.

[54]Neil Plantinga Jr., *Not the Way It's Supposed to Be: A Breviary of Sin* (Grand Rapids: Eerdmans, 1995).

[55]There has been some discussion as to whether disorders of sexual development or intersex conditions challenge the idea of ontological significance of male-female differences. Those who argue against ontological significance emphasize the sameness of males and females, pointing to how various intersex conditions remind us that genitalia, for example, comes from the same embryologic tissue. Megan K. DeFranza, *Intersex and Imago: Sex, Gender, and Sexuality in Postmodern Theological Anthropology* (PhD diss., Marquette University, 2011), http://epublications.marquette.edu/dissertations_mu/117. I think this is an important consideration, but one that does not exhaust the possibilities

here, as ontology also refers to the sorting of existing things. One can either highlight the differences between males/females and other aspects of creation, for example, or highlight the differences between males and females. Many would view intersex conditions as actually underscoring those differences at least in terms of how rare intersex conditions are (or, put differently, the frequency by which males and females develop without such complications).

[56]Looy, "Male and Female God Created Them," p. 11.

[57]Ibid.

[58]Lynn Conway has a helpful summary that includes historical and current global perspectives. See http://ai.eecs.umich.edu/people/conway/TS/TG-TS%20World.html#Hijra.

[59]Judith Butler, *Gender Trouble: Feminism and the Subversion of Identity* (New York: Routledge, 1990), p. 7. This perspective is steeped in queer theory, which is perhaps best understood as a philosophical commitment to epistemology (how we know things and what counts as knowledge) with a focus on deconstruction. See Kelby Harrison, *Sexual Deceit: The Ethics of Passing* (Lanham, MD: Lexington Books, 2013), pp. 93-111. For a critical evaluation of transgenderism from a feminist perspective, see Sheila Jeffreys, *Gender Hurts: A Feminist Critique of the Politics Behind Transgenderism* (New York: Routledge, 2014).

[60]International Gay and Lesbian Human Rights Commission [IGLHRC], Institutional Memoir of the 2005 Institute for Trans and Intersex Activist Training (2005): 7-8, https://iglhrc.org/sites/default/files/367-1.pdf.

[61]Adapted from Veronica R. F. Johnson and Mark A. Yarhouse, "Shame in Sexual Minorities: Stigma, Internal Cognitions, and Counseling Consideration," *Counseling and Values* 58, no. 1 (2013): 85.

[62]Mark A. Yarhouse and Trista L. Carr, "MtF Transgender Christians' Experiences: A Qualitative Study," *Journal of LGBT Issues in Counseling* 6, no. 1 (2012): 26.

[63]Jones, "Is Sex or Gender a Choice?"

[64]Ibid.

[65]Richard A. Carroll, "Gender Dysphoria," in *Principles and Practice of Sex Therapy,* 4th ed., ed. Sandra R. Leiblum (New York: Guilford, 2007).

[66]Melinda Selmys, personal communication, April 13, 2014.

[67]Jones, "Is Sex or Gender a Choice?"

CHAPTER 3: WHAT CAUSES GENDER DYSPHORIA?

[1]American Psychiatric Association, *The Diagnostic and Statistical Manual of Mental Disorders,* 5th ed. (Washington, DC: American Psychiatric Association, 2013), p. 452.

[2]Anne A. Lawrence, "Proposed Revisions to Gender Identity Disorder Diagnoses in the *DSM-5,*" *Archives of Sexual Behavior* 39 (2010): 1253-60.

[3]Tom Mazur and his colleagues make an interesting observation about conflating intersex conditions with gender dysphoria:

> Lumping individuals with intersex with those who are nonintersex but experiencing problems of gender, or who challenge conventional gender boundaries, enlarges the base of minorities, which, hopefully, increases their political influence and the opportunity to gain "rights" previously denied to them. Such blurring of distinctions and inconsistent language use for political (or other) uses can be advantageous; however, merging categories can complicate the work of both scientists and clinicians who are charged with the tasks of elucidating conditions' etiologies and developing effective treatment strategies.

Tom Mazur, Melissa Colsman and David E. Sandberg, "Intersex: Definition, Examples, Gender Stability and the Case Against Merging with Transsexualism," in *Principles of Transgender Medicine and Surgery*, ed. Randi Ettner, Stan Monstrey and A. Evan Eyler (New York: Hayworth, 2007), p. 254.

[4]Ibid., p. 254.

[5]This is an interesting development throughout several sections under the influence of the Sexual and Gender Identities Work Group for *DSM-5*. In the section on the paraphilias, a new distinction is made between the paraphilias and Paraphilic Disorders. A paraphilia reflects a sexual deviation or strong/intense atypical sexual interest. The *DSM-5* defines a paraphilia as "any intense and persistent sexual interest other than sexual interest in genital stimulation or preparatory fondling with phenotypically normal, physically mature, consenting human partners" (p. 685). A *Paraphilic Disorder* would distinguish those with a mental health issue, which appears to be reflected in whether they are distressed or impaired in some way. According to *DSM-5*, "A paraphilic disorder is a paraphilia that is currently causing distress or impairment to the individual or a paraphilia whose satisfaction has entailed personal harm, or risk of harm, to others" (pp. 685-86). This change reflects the ways in which sexual interests and behaviors are expanding to reflect a range of diverse interests, as well as the reluctance within the mental health field to identify patterns of behavior as reflecting mental health concerns unless the person is already distressed (ibid.). For a discussion of this change, see Mark A. Yarhouse and Erica S. N. Tan, *Sexuality and Sex Therapy: A Comprehensive Christian Appraisal* (Downers Grove, IL: IVP Academic, 2014).

[6]Kenneth J. Zucker, "Gender Identity Disorder in Children and Adolescents," *Annual Review of Clinical Psychology* 1 (2005): 477.

[7]Ibid.

[8]Richard A. Carroll, "Gender Dysphoria," in *Principles and Practice of Sex Therapy*, ed. Sandra R. Leiblum, 4th ed. (New York: Guilford, 2007), p. 479.

[9]Ibid.

[10]The *DSM-5* identifies Transvestic Disorder as the primary condition in which cross-dressing is associated with sexual arousal. It is the experience of adolescent or adult males "for whom cross-dressing behavior generates sexual excitement and causes distress and/or impairment without drawing their primary gender into question. It is oc-

casionally accompanied by gender dysphoria." It is a condition rarely diagnosed in females (p. 458).

The proposed *Guidelines for Psychological Practice with Transgender and Gender Non-Conforming Clients* note that the reference to Transvestites, which they define as "someone who wears clothing, jewelry and/or make-up and/or adopts a gender role expression not traditionally associated with a person's sex assigned at birth," is "controversial and is considered pejorative and outdated by some community members and professionals, instead preferring the term cross dresser" (*Guidelines for Psychological Practice with Transgender and Gender Non-Conforming Clients* proposed by the American Psychological Association, p. 12, temporarily posted on http://www.apa.org, retrieved May 27, 2014).

[11]Let me acknowledge that many transgender people would not include those who perform drag under the transgender umbrella. While I am sympathetic with the distinction that people want to make between drag and gender incongruence, other experts in this area have also listed those who perform drag as part of the transgender community. See, for example, Carroll, "Gender Dysphoria," p. 482.

The relationship between transgender persons and those who perform drag has recently been in the news with RuPaul receiving criticism for the use of the word "tranny." In a commentary by Parker Marie Molloy that appeared in *The Advocate*, Molloy wrote directly to RuPaul and shared: "The fact of the matter, Ru, is that words do hurt, and when you continue to use words that are frequently used to dehumanize people like me, that are used as precursors for assault, after you've been informed how hurtful these words are, you're no better than a racist who uses the '*n* word,' the homophobe who calls gay men 'faggots,' or the misogynist who refers to his female coworkers as 'bitches'" (Parker Marie Molloy, "It's Time to Stop with the *T* Word," *The Advocate*, February 20, 2014, www.advocate.com/commentary/2014/02/20/op-ed-its-time-stop-t-word).

[12]Cressida Heyes, "Identity Politics," in *The Stanford Encyclopedia of Philosophy*, Spring 2012 ed., ed. Edward N. Zalta, http://plato.stanford.edu/archives/spr2012/entries/identity-politics.

[13]Heyes, "Identity Politics."

[14]Ibid.

[15]Milton Diamond, "A Conversation with Dr. Milton Diamond," by Dean Kotula, 2002, http://www.hawaii.edu/PCSS/biblio/articles/2000to2004/2002-conversation.html.

[16]Cindy Meston and Penny Frohlich, "Gender Identity Disorder," http://homepage.psy.utexas.edu/HomePage/Group/MestonLAB/HTML%20files/Resources_msd_gender.htm.

[17]Dick F. Swaab and Alicia Garcia-Falgueras, "Sexual Differentiation of the Human Brain in Relation to Gender Identity and Sexual Orientation," *Functional Neurology* 24, no. 1 (2009): 18.

[18]Meston and Frohlich, "Gender Identity Disorder," http://homepage.psy.utexas.edu/HomePage/Group/MestonLAB/HTML%20files/Resources_msd_gender.htm.

[19]For example, R. Green and R. Young, "Hand Preference, Sexual Preference, and Trans-sexualism," *Archives of Sexual Behavior*, 30 (2001), pp. 565-74.

[20]For example, B. Kraemer, T. Noll, A. Delsignore, G. Milos, and U. Schnyder, "Finger Length Ratio (2D:4D) in Adults with Gender Identity Disorder," *Archives of Sexual Behavior*, 38 (3) (2009): pp. 359-63.

[21]Ibid. As the authors put it, "genetic females exposed to high levels of testosterone in utero (e.g., congential adrenal hyperplasia) rarely develop [gender dysphoria]." Furthermore, "prenatal exposure to antiandrogenic, androgenic, and estrogenic drugs rarely leads to [gender dysphoria] in either genetic females or males although some of these individuals display abnormal gender role behavior."

The experience of gender dysphoria varies among those who have an intersex condition. In a helpful review of the data, Tom Mazur and his colleagues offered the following observations about intersex conditions and gender dysphoria:

> (1) self-initiated gender change occurs in intersex syndromes and related conditions; (2) the prevalence of individuals who change gender varies by syndrome; (3) self-initiated gender change is not universal for any one syndrome or condition; (4) gender change is more frequent in XY persons than in those with an XX chromosomal pattern; (5) self-initiated gender change occurs in both directions, that is, male-to-female and female-to-male, although it more frequently occurs in the direction of female-to-male . . . ; and (6) there are no published reports of gender change in micropenis regardless of whether the person was assigned and reared as male or female. (From Mazur, Colsman and Sandberg, "Intersex," p. 247.)

[22]For example, J. N. Zhou, M. A. Hofman, L. J. G. Gooren and D. F. Swaab, "A Sex Difference in the Human Brain and Its Relation to Transsexuality," *Nature* 378 (1995): 68-70.

[23]For example, F. P. M. Kruijver, J. N. Zhou, C. W. Pool, M. A. Hofman, L. J. G. Gooren and D. F. Swaab, "Male-to-Female Transsexuals Have Female Neuron Numbers in a Limbic Nucleus," *The Journal of Clinical Endocrinology & Metabolism* 85, no. 5 (2000): 2034-41.

[24]Zhou, Hofman, Gooren and Swaab, "A Sex Difference in the Human Brain," pp. 68-70.

[25]Kruijver et al., "Male-to-Female Transsexuals Have Female Neuron Numbers in a Limbic Nucleus," pp. 2034-41.

[26]Zhou, Hofman, Gooren and Swaab, "A Sex Difference in the Human Brain," pp. 68-70.

[27]Wilson C. J. Chung, Geert J. DeVries and Dick F. Swaab, "Sexual Differentiation of the Bed Nucleus of the Stria Terminalis in Humans May Extend into Adulthood," *The Journal of Neuroscience* 22, no. 3 (February 1, 2002): 1027-33.

[28]Ibid., p. 1031.

[29]Critics of the brain-sex theory, such as Anne Lawrence, are not convinced. They note that these findings do not fit with the experience of gender dysphoria tracing back to childhood for most people.

[30]Chung et al., "Sexual Differentiation," p. 1032.

[31]See www.shb-info.org/sitebuildercontent/sitebuilderfiles/2_gooren_et_al.pdf.

[32]Milton Diamond, "Transsexuality Among Twins: Identity Concordance, Transition, Rearing, and Orientation," *International Journal of Transgenderism* 14, no. 1 (May 2013): 24-38.

[33]Milton Diamond, "Biased-Interaction of Psychosexual Development: 'How Does One Know if One Is Male or Female?'" *Sex Roles* 55 (2006): 5899-6000. Available online at www.hawaii.edu/PCSS/biblio/articles/2005to2009/2006-biased-interaction.html.

[34]Ibid. I have not focused as much on genetic contributions, but these are often discussed with reference to twin studies. In a recent study of transsexuality among twins that combined a convenience sample with past (largely convenience) samples, a 20 percent concordance rate was reported for all monozygotic twin pairs, which was more common among male twin pairs (33%) than female twin pairs (23%). Diamond, "Transsexuality Among Twins," pp. 24-38.

A relatively new topic in psychology and neuroscience is epigenetics, which considers whether any number of factors cause genes to be switched on or off in response to the environment. Proponents have turned to epigenetics to explain why one twin in a monozygotic twin pair might not be transsexual when the other twin is transsexual. See G. Dorner, F. Gotz, W. Rohde, A. Plagemann, R. Lindner, H. Peters and Z. Ghanaati, "Genetic and Epigenetic Effects on Sexual Brain Organization Mediated by Sex Hormones," *Neuroendocrinology Letters* 22, no. 6 (2001): 403-9.

For research on transsexuality among non-twin siblings in which siblings (particularly brothers) of transsexual persons have a higher chance of being transsexual than the general population, see E. Gomez-Gill, I. Esteva, M. C. Almaraz, E. Pasaro, S. Segovia and A. Guillamon, "Familiarity of Gender Identity Disorders in Non-twin Siblings," *Archives of Sexual Behavior* 39 (2010): 546-52.

[35]Diamond, "Biased-Interaction of Psychosexual Development," www.hawaii.edu/PCSS/biblio/articles/2005to2009/2006-biased-interaction.html.

[36]Ibid.

[37]Ibid.

[38]Kruijver et al., "Male-to-Female Transsexuals Have Female Neuron Numbers in a Limbic Nucleus," pp. 2034-41; Zhou, Hofman, Gooren and Swaab, "A Sex Difference in the Human Brain," pp. 68-70.

[39]Zhou, Hofman, Gooren and Swaab, "A Sex Difference in the Human Brain," pp. 68-70.

[40]The Kruijver et al. study used the same six MtF transsexuals as were used by the Zhou et al. team and added one additional MtF transsexual. See Michael Bailey, http://gendertrender.wordpress.com/2012/11/21/what-many-transgender-activists-dont-want-you-to-know-and-why-you-should-know-it-anyway.

[41]Zhou, Hofman, Gooren and Swaab, "A Sex Difference in the Human Brain," p. 70.

[42]See http://gendertrender.wordpress.com/2012/11/21/what-many-transgender-activists-dont-want-you-to-know-and-why-you-should-know-it-anyway.

[43]See also Eileen Luders, Francisco J. Sanchez, Christian Gaser, Arthur W. Toga, Katherine L. Narr, Liberty S. Hamilton and Eric Vilain, "Regional Gray Matter Variation in Male-to-Female Transsexualism," *NeuroImage* 46 (2009): 904-7.

[44]William M. Struthers, personal communication, January 6, 2014.

[45]See an interesting study of regional blood flow changes among female-to-male transsexuals by Hideyuki Nawata, Koji Ogomori, Mariko Tanaka, Ryoji Nishimura, Hajime Urashima, Rika Yano, Koichi Takano and Yasuo Kuwabara, "Regional Cerebral Blood Flow Change in Female to Male Gender Identity Disorder," *Psychiatry and Clinical Neurosciences* 64 (2010): 157-61.

[46]William M. Struthers, personal communication, January 6, 2014.

[47]Lawrence, in "Proposed Revisions to Gender Identity Disorder Diagnoses in the *DSM-5*," argues that dissatisfaction with subtypes based on sexual orientation appears to be related to activism/nonscientific dissatisfaction with that particular typology.

[48]Anne A. Lawrence, "Factors Associated with Satisfaction or Regret Following Male-to-Female Sex Reassignment Surgery," *Archives of Sexual Behavior* 32, no. 4 (2003): 300.

[49]Ibid. See also Anne A. Lawrence, "Transgenderism in Nonhomosexual Males as a Paraphilic Phenomenon: Implications for Case Conceptualization and Treatment," *Sexual and Relationship Therapy* 24, no. 2 (2009): 188-206.

[50]Ray Blanchard, "Gender Identity Disorders in Adult Men," in *Clinical Management of Gender Identity Disorders in Children and Adults*, ed. R. Blanchard and B. V. Steiner (Washington, DC: American Psychiatric Publishing, 1990), pp. 49-75; Ray Blanchard, "Gender Identity Disorders in Adult Women," in *Clinical Management of Gender Identity Disorders in Children and Adults*, ed. R. Blanchard and B. V. Steiner (Washington, DC: American Psychiatric Publishing, 1990), pp. 77-91.

[51]Blanchard, "Gender Identity Disorders in Adult Men." Among those who would fall into an autogynephilic presentation, Blanchard suggested a range of experiences: transvestic, anatomic, physiologic and behavioral. See also Anne Lawrence, *Men Trapped in Women's Bodies: Narratives of Autogynephilic Transsexualism* (New York: Springer, 2013).

[52]See http://gendertrender.wordpress.com/2012/11/21/what-many-transgender-activists-dont-want-you-to-know-and-why-you-should-know-it-anyway.

[53]See http://ai.eecs.umich.edu/people/conway/TS/LynnsReviewOfBaileysBook.html.

[54]See http://gendertrender.wordpress.com/2012/11/21/what-many-transgender-activists-dont-want-you-to-know-and-why-you-should-know-it-anyway.

[55]For a discussion of this decision, see Lawrence, "Proposed Revisions to Gender Identity Disorder Diagnoses in the *DSM-5*," p. 1258.

[56]Robert J. Stoller, "The hermaphroditic identity of hermaphrodites," *Journal of Nervous and Mental Disease*, 139 (1964), pp. 453-57.

[57]Lawrence Kohlberg, "A Cognitive-Developmental Analysis of Children's Sex-Role Concepts and Attitudes," *The Development of Sex Differences*, ed. E. E. Maccody (Stanford, CA: Stanford University Press), pp. 82-173.

[58]Zucker, "Gender Identity Disorder in Children and Adolescents," p. 468.

[59]H. F. L. Meyer-Bahlburg, "Gender Identity Disorder in Young Boys: A Parent- and Peer-Based Treatment Protocol," *Clinical Child Psychology and Psychiatry* 7, no. 3 (2002): 360-76.

[60]Ibid., p. 363.

[61]J. F. Veale, D. E. Clarke and T. C. Lomax, "Biological and Psychosocial Correlates of Adult Gender Variant Identities: A Review," *Personality and Individual Differences* 48 (2009): 357-66.

[62]For example, see P. T. Cohen-Kettenis and W. A. Arrindell, "Perceived Parental Rearing Style, Parental Divorce and Transsexualism: A Controlled Study," *Psychological Medicine* 20 (1990): 613-20; M. Hogan-Finlay, *Development of the Cross Gender Lifestyle and Comparison of Cross Gendered Men with Heterosexual Controls* (PhD diss., Carleton University, Ottawa, Canada, 1995); R. L. Schott, "The Childhood and Family Dynamics of Transvestites," *Archives of Sexual Behavior* 24 (1995): 309-27.

[63]Veale, Clarke and Lomax, "Biological and Psychosocial Correlates of Adult Gender Variant Identities," 357-66; D. Gehring and G. Knudson, "Prevalence of Childhood Trauma in a Clinical Population of Transsexual People," *International Journal of Transgenderism* 8 (2005): 23-30.

[64]Meyer-Bahlburg, "Gender Identity Disorder in Young Boys," p. 364.

[65]Ibid.

[66]P. T. Cohen-Kettenis and L. J. G. Gooren, "Transsexualism: A Review of Etiology, Diagnosis and Treatment," *Journal of Psychosomatic Research*, 46 (4) (1999), pp. 315-33.

[67]Kenneth J. Zucker and Susan L. Bradley, "Gender Identity and Psychosexual Disorders," *The American Psychiatric Publishing Textbook of Child and Adolescent Psychiatry*, eds. J. Wiener and M. Dulcan (Washington, DC: American Psychiatric Publishing, 2004), pp. 813-35.

[68]Kenneth J. Zucker and Nicola Brown, "Gender Dysphoria," in *Principles and Practice of Sex Therapy*, 5th ed., eds. Yitzchak M. Binik and Kathryn S. K. Hall (New York: Guilford, 2014), p. 243.

[69]Kenneth J. Zucker, "DSM-5: Call for Commentaries on Gender Dysphoria, Sexual Dysfunctions, and Paraphilic Disorders," *Archives of Sexual Behavior*, 42(5) (2013), pp. 669-74.

[70]Meyer-Bahlburg, "Gender Identity Disorder in Young Boys," p. 472.

[71]This seems consistent with theorists who believe that "the most likely developmental pathway to [gender dysphoria] will involve temperamental features coupled with a variety of psychosocial risk factors which in aggregate determine how far the child moves into the cross-gender area" (Ibid., p. 364).

CHAPTER 4: PHENOMENOLOGY AND PREVALENCE

[1]Richard A. Carroll, "Assessment and Treatment of Gender Dysphoria," in *Principles and Practice of Sex Therapy*, 3rd ed., ed. S. R. Leiblum and R. C. Rosen (New York: Guilford, 2000), p. 369.

[2]American Psychiatric Association, *Diagnostic and Statistical Manual of Mental Disorders,* 5th ed. (Washington, DC: American Psychiatric Publishing, 2013), p. 452.

[3]Ibid.

[4]John Colapinto, *As Nature Made Him: The Boy Who Was Raised as a Girl* (New York: HarperCollins, 2000).

[5]T. D. Steensma, R. Biemond, F. deBoer and P. T. Cohen-Kettenis, "Desisting and Persisting Gender Dysphoria After Childhood: A Qualitative Study," *Clinical Child Psychology and Psychiatry* (2010): 1-18.

[6]Ibid., p. 5.

[7]Ibid.

[8]Ibid., p. 7.

[9]Ibid.

[10]American Psychiatric Association, *Diagnostic Statistical Manual of Mental Disorders,* 5th ed. (Washington, DC: American Psychiatric Publishing, 2013), p. 452.

[11]See, for example, www.ag.gov.au/Publications/Pages/AustralianGovernmentGuidelines ontheRecognitionofSexandGender.aspx. Also, in 2013 Germany officially sanctioned the designation "indeterminate gender" on birth certificates for babies whose gender was unable to be assigned at birth.

[12]Steensma, Biemond, deBoer and Cohen-Kettenis, "Desisting and Persisting Gender Dysphoria After Childhood," pp. 1-18.

[13]Ibid., p. 7.

[14]Ibid.

[15]Kenneth J. Zucker, "Gender Identity Disorder in Children and Adolescents," *Annual Review of Clinical Psychology 1,* no. 1 (2005): 467-92.

[16]*DSM-5,* p. 455.

[17]Zucker, "Gender Identity Disorder in Children and Adolescents," p. 473.

[18]See Kenneth J. Zucker and Susan J. Bradley, "Gender Identity and Psychosexual Disorders," *Focus 3,* no. 4 (2005): 598-617.

[19]*DSM-5,* p. 454.

[20]J. R. Blosnich, G. R. Brown, J. C. Shipherd, M. Kauth, R. I. Piegari and R. M. Bossarte, "Prevalence of Gender Identity Disorder and Suicide Risk Among Transgender Veterans Utilizing Veterans Health Administration Care," *American Journal of Public Health 103, no. 1* (2013): e27-e32; see also A. Bakker, P. J. M. van Kesteren, L. Gooren and P. Bezemer, "The Prevalence of Transsexualism in the Netherlands," *Acta Psychiatr Scand 87, no. 4* (1993): 237-38; G. DeCuypere, M. van Hemellrijck, A. Michel et al., "Prevalence and Demography of Transsexualism in Belgium," *European Psychiatry 22,* no. 3 (2007): 137-41.

[21]K. J. Conron, G. Scott, G. S. Stowell, and S. J. Landers, "Transgender Health in Massachusetts: Results from a Household Probability Sample of Adults," *American Journal of Public Health,* 102(1) (2012), pp. 118-22; Gary J. Gates, "How Many People are Gay, Bisexual, and Transgender?" The Williams Institute, April 2011, pp. 1-8. Available: http://

williamsinstitute.law.ucla.edu/wp-content/uploads/Gates-How-Many-People-LGBT
-Apr-2011.pdf.

[22]Kenneth J. Zucker and Nicola Brown, "Gender Dysphoria," in *Principles and Practice of Sex Therapy*, 5th ed., ed. Yitzchak M. Binik and Kathryn S. K. Hall (New York: Guilford, 2014), p. 238.

[23]Zucker, "Gender Identity Disorder in Children and Adolescents," pp. 467-92.

[24]For a discussion of this, see Mark A. Yarhouse, Richard E. Butman and Barrett W. McRay, *Modern Psychopathologies: A Comprehensive Christian Appraisal* (Downers Grove, IL: InterVarsity Press, 2005), pp. 58-80.

[25]Zucker, "Gender Identity Disorder in Children and Adolescents," p. 477.

[26]Ibid.

[27]Carroll, "Assessment and Treatment of Gender Dysphoria," pp. 368-422.

[28]James T. Kimber, "Types of Crossdressers: A Typology of Transgender Persons with Behaviorally Significant Amounts of Internal Motivation," unpublished manuscript.

[29]Ray Blanchard, "Gender Identity Disorders in Adult Men," in *Clinical Management of Gender Identity Disorders in Children and Adults*, ed. Ray Blanchard and B. V. Steiner (Washington, DC: American Psychiatric Publishing, 1990), pp. 49-75; Ray Blanchard, "Gender Identity Disorders in Adult Women," in *Clinical Management of Gender Identity Disorders in Children and Adults* (Washington, DC: American Psychiatric Publishing, 1990), pp. 77-91.

[30]Blanchard, "Gender Identity Disorders in Adult Women," p. 81.

[31]Blanchard, "Gender Identity Disorders in Adult Men," pp. 49-75.

[32]Ibid., p. 71.

[33]Ibid., pp. 49-75.

[34]Carroll, "Assessment and Treatment of Gender Dysphoria," pp. 368-422.

[35]Ibid., p. 377.

[36]Anne A. Lawrence, *Men Trapped in Women's Bodies: Narratives of Autogynephilic Transsexualism* (New York: Springer, 2013), p. 2.

[37]Ibid., p. 3.

[38]Blanchard, "Gender Identity Disorders in Adult Men," p. 58.

[39]Lawrence, *Men Trapped in Women's Bodies*, p. 95.

[40]Blanchard, "Gender Identity Disorders in Adult Men," pp. 49-75.

[41]Zucker and Brown, "Gender Dysphoria," p. 251.

[42]Ibid., pp. 251-52.

CHAPTER 5: PREVENTION AND TREATMENT OF GENDER DYSPHORIA

[1]T. D. Steensma, R. Biemond, F. deBoer and P. T. Cohen-Kettenis, "Desisting and Persisting Gender Dysphoria After Childhood: A Qualitative Study," *Clinical Child Psychology and Psychiatry* (2010): 1-18.

[2]See, for example, Jack Drescher, "Controversies in gender diagnoses," *LGBT Health* 1, no. 1 (2014): 13.

[3]H. F. L. Meyer-Bahlburg, "Gender Identity Disorder in Young Boys: A Parent- and Peer-Based Treatment Protocol," *Clinical Child Psychology and Psychiatry* 7, no. 3 (2002): 360-76.

[4]Ibid., p. 361.

[5]Kenneth J. Zucker, "Gender Identity Disorder in Children and Adolescents," *Treatments of Psychiatric Disorders*, 3rd ed., ed. G. Gabbard (Washington, DC: American Psychiatric Press, 2001), pp. 2069-94; Kenneth J. Zucker and Susan L. Bradley, *Gender Identity Disorder and Psychosexual Problems in Children and Adolescents* (New York and London: The Guilford Press, 1995).

[6]Zucker, "Gender Identity Disorder in Children and Adolescents;" see also Meyer-Bahlburg, "Gender Identity Disorder in Young Boys."

[7]H. F. L. Meyer-Bahlburg, "Gender Identity Disorder in Young Boys: A Parent- and Peer-Based Treatment Protocol," *Clinical Child Psychology and Psychiatry*, 7 (2002), pp. 360-77; Zucker, "Gender Identity Disorder in Children and Adolescents."

[8]Zucker, "Gender Identity Disorder in Children and Adolescents;" Kenneth J. Zucker, "Gender Identity Development and Issues," *Child and Adolescent Psychiatric Clinics of North America*, 13 (2004), pp. 551-68.

[9]Meyer-Bahlburg, "Gender Identity Disorder in Young Boys: A Parent- and Peer-Based Treatment Protocol," p. 365.

[10]Zucker, "Gender Identity Disorder in Children and Adolescents."

[11] Meyer-Bahlburg, "Gender Identity Disorder in Young Boys;" Zucker, "Gender Identity Disorder in Children and Adolescents;" Zucker, "Gender Identity Development and Issues."

[12]Meyer-Bahlburg, "Gender Identity Disorder in Young Boys," pp. 360-76.

[13]Alix Spiegel, "Parents Consider Treatment to Delay Son's Puberty," National Public Radio, May 8, 2008. Available at: http://www.npr.org/templates/story/story.php?storyId=90273278.

[14]American Psychiatric Association, *Diagnostic and Statistical Manual of Mental Disorders*, 5th ed. (Washington, DC: American Psychiatric Publishing, 2013).

[15]Steensma, Biemond, deBoer and Cohen-Kettenis, "Desisting and Persisting Gender Dysphoria After Childhood," pp. 1-18.

[16]Ibid., p. 13.

[17]Ibid.

[18]Drescher, "Controversies in Gender Diagnoses," pp. 10-14.

[19]See www.nytimes.com/2013/06/30/opinion/sunday/sunday-dialogue-our-notions-of-gender.html?pagewanted=all&_r=1&.

[20]J. Olson, C. Forbes, and M. Belzer, "Management of the Transgender Adolescent," *Archives of Pediatrics and Adolescent Medicine*, 165 (2) (2011), pp. 171-76.

[21]Drescher, "Controversies in Gender Diagnoses," pp. 10-14.

[22]Olson, Forbes and Belzer, "Management of the Transgender Adolescent," p. 173.

[23]Ibid., p. 174.

[24]See www.npr.org/templates/story/story.php?storyId=90273278.

[25]Spiegel, "Parents Consider Treatment to Delay Son's Puberty."

[26]See also deVries, Steensma, Doreleijers and Cohen-Kettenis, 2011, B. P. Kreukels and P. T. Cohen-Kettenis, "Puberty Suppression in Gender Identity Disorder: The Amsterdam Experience," *National Review of Endocrinology*, 17 (7) (2011), pp. 466-72.

[27]Kreukels and Cohen-Kettenis, "Puberty Suppression in Gender Identity Disorder: The Amsterdam Experience."

[28]In the same NPR report, it was noted that "taking testosterone or estrogen immediately after blocking puberty will make a teenage patient sterile." Spack shared, "This is one of the most controversial aspects of this. At what age can a young person fully understand the implications of doing something that will make fertility for them, by today's technology, virtually impossible?" Spack also noted that "there is no risk of infertility from the hormone-blocking treatment alone. Infertility only comes when the hormone-blocking treatment is paired with Stage 2, the use of opposite-sex hormones. And so, Spack says, hormone blockers should really be seen simply as a treatment that gives families more time to think about what to do" (www.npr.org/templates/story/story.php?storyId=90273278).

[29]Kreukels and Cohen-Kettenis, "Puberty Suppression in Gender Identity Disorder: The Amsterdam Experience."

[30]See Eli Coleman, W. Bockting, M. Cohen-Kettenis et al., "Standards of Care for the Health of Transsexual, Transgender, and Gender-Nonconforming People, Version 7," *International Journal of Transgenderism* 13 (2011): 174-75.

[31]Zucker, "Gender Identity Disorder in Children and Adolescents."

[32]Ibid., p. 285.

[33]Zucker, "Gender Identity Development and Issues."

[34]Olson, Forbes and Belzer, "Management of the Transgender Adolescent."

[35]Ibid.

[36]Richard Carroll, "Assessment and Treatment of Gender Dysphoria," in *Principles and Practice of Sex Therapy*, 3rd ed., ed. S. R. Leiblum and R. C. Rosen (New York: Guilford, 2000), pp. 368-422.

[37]Ibid., p. 380; Richard Carroll, "Gender Dysphoria and Transgender Experiences," in *Principles and Practice of Sex Therapy*, 4th ed., ed. S. R. Leiblum (New York: Guilford, 2007), pp. 477-508. For the Standards of Care, see www.wpath.org.

[38]Carroll, "Gender Dysphoria and Transgender Experiences," p. 490.

[39]Ibid., p. 380.

[40]Ibid., p. 491.

[41]Ibid.

[42]Ibid.

[43]Ibid.

[44]Some prefer to use the term "gender-affirming surgery" rather than "sex reassignment" or "gender reassignment." See American Psychological Association's proposed *Guidelines for Psychological Practice with Transgender and Gender Non-Conforming Clients*, p. 6; temporarily posted at http://www.apa.org, retrieved May 27, 2014.

[45]The Standards of Care are updated and currently available at www.wpath.org. Guidelines for hormonal treatment are published by the Endocrine Society. See "Endocrine Treatment of Transsexual Persons: An Endocrine Society Clinical Practice Guideline," first published in the *Journal of Clinical Endocrinology & Metabolism*, September 2009, 94(9), pp. 3132–54, https://www.endocrine.org/~/media/endosociety/Files/Publications/Clinical%20Practice%20Guidelines/Endocrine-Treatment-of-Transsexual-Persons.pdf.

[46]Coleman, "Standards of Care," p. 183.

[47]Ibid.

[48]Ibid., p. 184.

[49]Carroll, "Assessment and Treatment of Gender Dysphoria," pp. 368-422; Carroll, "Gender Dysphoria and Transgender Experiences," p. 491.

[50]Coleman, "Standards of Care," p. 183.

[51]Ibid., p. 202.

[52]Ibid.

[53]A. I. Lev, "Transgender Communities: Developing Identity Through Connection," in *Handbook of Counseling and Psychotherapy with Lesbian, Gay, Bisexual and Transgender Clients*, 2nd ed., ed. K. J. Bieschke, R. M. Perez and K. A. DeBord (Washington, DC: American Psychological Association, 2007), pp. 147-75.

[54]Trista L. Carr, Mark A. Yarhouse and Rebecca L. Thomas, "MtF Transgender Christians: An Exploratory Study with Milestone Events," poster presentation at the National Transgender Health Summit, Oakland, California, May 17-18, 2013. See also Trista L. Carr, Mark A. Yarhouse and Rebecca Thomas, "Report on TG Christians' milestone events," in Beverly Miller, *Gender Identity: Disorders, Developmental Perspectives and Social Implications* (New York: Nova Science Publishers, in press).

[55]Tom Mazur, Melissa Colsman and David E. Sandberg, "Intersex: Definition, Examples, Gender Stability and the Case Against Merging with Transsexualism," in *Principles of Transgender Medicine and Surgery*, ed. Randi Ettner, Stan Monstrey and A. Evan Eyler (New York: Hayworth, 2007), p. 251.

[56]Carroll, "Gender Dysphoria and Transgender Experiences," pp. 477-508.

[57]Carroll, "Assessment and Treatment of Gender Dysphoria," pp. 368-422. See also Luk Gijs and Anne Brewaeys, "Surgical Treatment of Gender Dysphoria in Adults and Adolescents: Recent Developments, Effectiveness, and Challenges," *Annual Review of Sex Research*, 18 (1) (2007), pp. 178-224, REF; A. J. Kuiper and P. T. Cohen-Kettenis, "Sex Reassignment Surgery: A study of 141 Dutch Transsexuals," *Archives of Sexual Behavior*,

17 (1988), pp. 439-57.

[58]Zucker and Brown, "Gender Dysphoria," p. 257.

[59]C. Dhejne, O. Öberg, S.Arver and M. Landén, "An Analysis of All Applications for Sex Reassignment Surgery in Sweden, 1960–2010: Prevalence, Incidence, and Regrets," *Archives of Sexual Behavior* 43, no. 8 (2014): 1535-45.

[60]Ibid., p. 249. As Zucker and Brown note, the current Standards of Care have moved away from the language of "real-life experience," viewing it as coming across as too "paternalistic" and creating "undue hardship"; instead, the current language is that of "a continuous gender-role experience for genital surgery only, opening up alternatives for people to document their lives and understanding of the social consequences of transition, offering time to adjust and adapt to the challenges inherent within" (pp. 249-50).

[61]Carroll, "Assessment and Treatment of Gender Dysphoria." See also Anne A. Lawrence, "Factors Associated with Satisfaction or Regret Following Male-to-Female Sex Reassignment Surgery," *Archives of Sexual Behavior* 32, no. 4 (2003): 299-315.

[62]Blanchard, "Gender Identity Disorders in Adult Men," p. 59.

[63]Anne A. Lawrence, *Men Trapped in Women's Bodies: Narratives of Autogynephilic Transsexualism* (New York: Springer, 2013).

[64]Carroll, "Gender Dysphoria and Transgender Experiences," pp. 477-508.

[65]See A. Johansson, E. Sundborn, T. Hojerback and O. Bodlund, "A Five-Year Follow-Up Study of Swedish Adults with Gender Identity Disorder," *Archives of Sexual Behavior* 39 (2010): 1429-37; Louis J. Gooren, Erik J. Giltay and Matthijs C. Bunck, "Long-Term Treatment of Transsexuals with Cross-Sex Hormones: Extensive Personal Experience," *Journal of Clinical Endocrinol Metabolism* 93, no. 1 (2008): 19-25.

[66]Cecilia Dhejne, Paul Lichtenstein, Marcus Boman, Anna L. V. Johansson, Niklas Langstrom, Mikael Landen, "Long-Term Follow-Up of Transsexual Persons Undergoing Sex Reassignment Surgery: Cohort Study in Sweden," *PLoS ONE* 6, no. 2 (2011): e16995. Doi: 10.1371/journal.pone.0016885. See also Annette Kuhn, Christine Bodmer, Werner Stadlmayr, Peter Kuhn, Michael D. Mueller and Martin Birkhauser, "Quality of Life 15 Years After Sex Reassignment Surgery for Transsexualism," *Fertility and Sterility* 92, no. 5 (2009): 1685-89.

[67]Dhejne et al., "Long-Term Follow-Up of Transsexual Persons Undergoing Sex Reassignment Surgery: Cohort Study in Sweden," p. 7.

[68]Ibid.

[69]Paul R. McHugh, "Psychiatric Misadventures," *American Scholar* 61, no. 4 (1992): 502.

[70]Ibid., p. 503.

[71]Ibid.

[72]Paul McHugh, "Transgender Surgery Isn't the Solution," *The Wall Street Journal*, June 12, 2014, http://online.wsj.com/articles/paul-mchugh-transgender-surgery-isnt-the-solution-1402615120. These are powerful images. However, in a recent discussion about this parallel a colleague mentioned that the professional consensus around the etiology

of anorexia is that while causal pathways are multifaceted, it is one of the mental health issues believed to be most influenced by culture in terms of beauty/self-worth, perfectionism and competition. It is unclear that environmental influences on Gender Dysphoria would function in any way similar to what we see in the various eating disorders.

[73]Kevin D. Williams, "Laverne Cox Is Not a Woman: Facts Are Not Subject to Our Feelings," *The Chicago Sun-Times*, May 30, 2014. Although printed and subsequently retracted, the original article is available here: www.nationalreview.com/article/379188/laverne-cox-not-woman-kevin-d-williamson. The fact that the article was officially retracted gives the reader a sense of what is open to debate in our current cultural discourse on gender identity.

[74]McHugh, "Psychiatric Misadventures," p. 503.

[75]Lawrence, *Men Trapped in Women's Bodies.*

CHAPTER 6: TOWARD A CHRISTIAN RESPONSE: AT THE LEVEL OF THE INDIVIDUAL

[1]J. L. Zimmerman and V. C. Dickerson, "Using a Narrative Metaphor: Implications for Theory and Clinical Practice," *Family Process*, 33 (3) (1994), pp. 233-45.

[2]Ibid., p. 235.

[3]Mark A. Yarhouse, Trista L. Carr and Emma Bucher, *Gender Identity Journeys* (Virginia Beach, VA: Institute for the Study of Sexual Identity, 2014).

[4]Ibid., p. 43.

[5]Ibid., pp. 45-46.

[6]Anne A. Lawrence, *Men Trapped in Women's Bodies: Narratives of Autogynephilic Transsexualism* (New York: Springer, 2013), p. 27.

[7]Ibid.

[8]Stanton L. Jones, "Is Sex or Gender a Choice?," in forthcoming *Holman Worldview Study Bible.*

[9]M. Griffith, "Opening Therapy to Conversations with a Personal God," *Spiritual Resources in Family Therapy*, ed. Froma Walsh (New York: The Guilford Press, 1999), pp. 209-22.

[10]Ibid.

[11]Yarhouse, Carr and Bucher, *Gender Identity Journeys*, p. 65.

[12]Ibid., pp. 64-65.

[13]Mark Yarhouse and Trista L. Carr, "MtF Transgender Christians' Experiences: A Qualitative study," *Journal of LGBT Issues in Counseling* 6, no. 1 (2012): 18-33. See also Trista L. Carr, Mark A. Yarhouse and Rebecca L. Thomas, "MtF Transgender Christians: An Exploratory Study with Milestone Events," poster presentation at the National Transgender Health Summit, Oakland, California, May 17-18, 2013.

[14]Ibid., p. 24.

[15]Ibid.

[16]Ibid., p. 25.

[17]Oliver O'Donovan, *Resurrection and Moral Order: An Outline for Evangelical Ethics*, 2nd ed. (Grand Rapids: Eerdmans, 1994), p. 260.

[18]Ibid.

[19]Ibid., p. 262.

[20]An exchange between two social conservatives on *Crosstalk* touched on the experience of transsexuals in the US military:

> I can only imagine the confusion that would be there if here is some guy dressed in a big skirt trying to look feminine climbing into the left seat in a bomber or into a jetfighter and getting his dress all snarled up trying to climb in. We're talking about guys running jackhammers and making bunkers and things like that, if there's anything disgusting it's to see, and I mean this kindly but women are made of God to be very special, and one day I was driving down the street and I saw this, well this lady was pretty hefty, but she was operating a jackhammer and what it did to her was absolutely astounding, it was wicked, it was a violation of the very purpose of the wonderful gift of femininity.
>
> If we've got people here now suddenly all on the altar of being able to—it's not just the transgenders [*sic*], now if you feel like you're feminine one day and feel like you're masculine the next day, you can change back and forth, switch-hitter. (www.vcyamerica.org/blog/2014/04/08/the-price-of-citizenship)

[21]O'Donovan, *Resurrection and Moral Order*, p. 264.

CHAPTER 7: TOWARD A CHRISTIAN RESPONSE: AT THE LEVEL OF THE INSTITUTION

[1]See www.theclause.org/2013/09/theology-professor-to-leave-university-over-transgender -identity.

[2]Elizabeth Redden, "Spring Arbor and Transgender Dean Settle," *Inside Higher Ed*, March 14, 2007, www.insidehighered.com/news/2007/03/14/springarbor.

[3]Sarah Pulliam Bailey, "Transgender Student Denied On-Campus Male Housing at Christian University," *Religion News Service*, April 9, 2014, www.religionnews.com/2014/04/09 /transgender-student-denied-campus-male-housing-christian-university.

[4]Representatives attending the Southern Baptist Convention recently adopted a resolution titled "On Transgender Identity" that reflected on cultural changes, such as the removal of Gender Identity Disorder from *DSM-5*, trends in services to gender dysphoric persons (such as "cross-sex hormone therapy, gender reassignment surgery, and social and legal transition to the desired gender"), and affirmations and accommodations based on a person's "self-perception of [his or her] own gender." The resolution affirms that gender identity is "determined by biological sex and not by one's self-perception"; "the reality of human fallenness which can result in such biological manifestations as intersexuality or psychological manifestations as gender identity con-

fusion"; "efforts to alter one's bodily identity (e.g., cross-sex hormone therapy, gender reassignment surgery) to refashion it to conform with one's perceived gender identity"; and "oppose steadfastly all efforts by any governing official or body to validate trans-gender identity as morally praiseworthy." There are also several affirmations of trans-gender persons as made in the image of God that include the denunciation of abuse toward transgender persons ("we regard our transgender neighbors as image-bearers of Almighty God and therefore condemn acts of abuse or bullying committed against them") and affirmations of transgender persons as welcome in church ("we love our transgender neighbors, seek their good always, welcome them to our churches and, as they repent and believe in Christ, receive them into church membership"). See www.sbc .net/resolutions/2250/on-transgender-identity.

[5]"Belong, Believe, Become," The Surprising God (blog), August 31, 2008, http:// thesurprisinggodblog.gci.org/2008/08/belong-believe-behave.html.

[6]Ibid.

[7]Mark A. Yarhouse and Trista L. Carr, "MtF Transgender Christians' Experiences: A Qualitative Study," *Journal of LGBT Issues in Counseling* 6, no. 1 (2012): 26.

[8]Cressida Heyes, "Identity Politics," *The Stanford Encyclopedia of Philosophy*, ed. Edward N. Zalta (spring 2012): http://plato.stanford.edu/archives/spr2012/entries/identity -politics. Heyes goes on to note: "What is crucial about the 'identity' of identity politics appears to be the experience of the subject, especially his or her experience of oppression and the possibility of a shared and more authentic or self-determined alternative. Thus identity politics rests on unifying claims about the meaning of politically laden experi-ences to diverse individuals."

[9]Ibid.

[10]Richard A. Carroll, "Gender Dysphoria and Transgender Experiences," in *Principles and Practice of Sex Therapy*, 4th ed., ed. S. R. Leiblum (New York: Guilford, 2007), pp. 477-508.

Index

CAPS
INTERNATIONAL

An Association for Christian Psychologists,
Therapists, Counselors and Academicians

CAPS is a vibrant Christian organization with a rich tradition. Founded in 1956 by a small group of Christian mental health professionals, chaplains and pastors, CAPS has grown to more than 2,100 members in the U.S., Canada and more than 25 other countries.

CAPS encourages in-depth consideration of therapeutic, research, theoretical and theological issues. The association is a forum for creative new ideas. In fact, their publications and conferences are the birthplace for many of the formative concepts in our field today.

CAPS members represent a variety of denominations, professional groups and theoretical orientations; yet all are united in their commitment to Christ and to professional excellence.

CAPS is a non-profit, member-supported organization. It is led by a fully functioning board of directors, and the membership has a voice in the direction of CAPS.

CAPS is more than a professional association. It is a fellowship, and in addition to national and international activities, the organization strongly encourages regional, local and area activities which provide networking and fellowship opportunities as well as professional enrichment.

To learn more about CAPS, visit www.caps.net.

The joint publishing venture between IVP Academic and CAPS aims to promote the understanding of the relationship between Christianity and the behavioral sciences at both the clinical/counseling and the theoretical/research levels. These books will be of particular value for students and practitioners, teachers and researchers.

For more information about CAPS Books, visit InterVarsity Press's website at www.ivpress.com/cgi-ivpress/book.pl/code=2801.

Other Books by Mark A. Yarhouse

Counseling Couples in Conflict
978-0-8308-3925-4

Family Therapies
978-0-8308-2805-0

Modern Psychopathologies
978-0-8308-6473-7

Sexuality and Sex Therapy
978-0-8308-6483-6

Finding the Textbook You Need

The IVP Academic Textbook Selector
is an online tool for instantly finding the IVP books
suitable for over 250 courses across 24 disciplines.

www.ivpress.com/academic/